MW00737576

ALSO BY THE AUTHOR

Two and Two Halves to Bhutan

Doctor on Everest

Backcountry Medical Guide/Far From Help

Atlin's Gold

Eric Shipton: Everest and Beyond
Winner of the Boardman Tasker international
prize for mountain literature

The Man Who Mapped the Arctic: The Intrepid Life of George Back, Franklin's Lieutenant.
A Globe and Mail and Amazon.ca Book of the Year

Over the Hills

And Far Away

SARAH
A LOVE STORY

BY

PETER STEELE

SARAH
A LOVE STORY

Cover design by Keara Hlewka
Author photo by Cathie Archbould
Computer consultant: Sasha Masson

ISBN: 978-0-9940614-4-7

peter.steele@northwestel.net

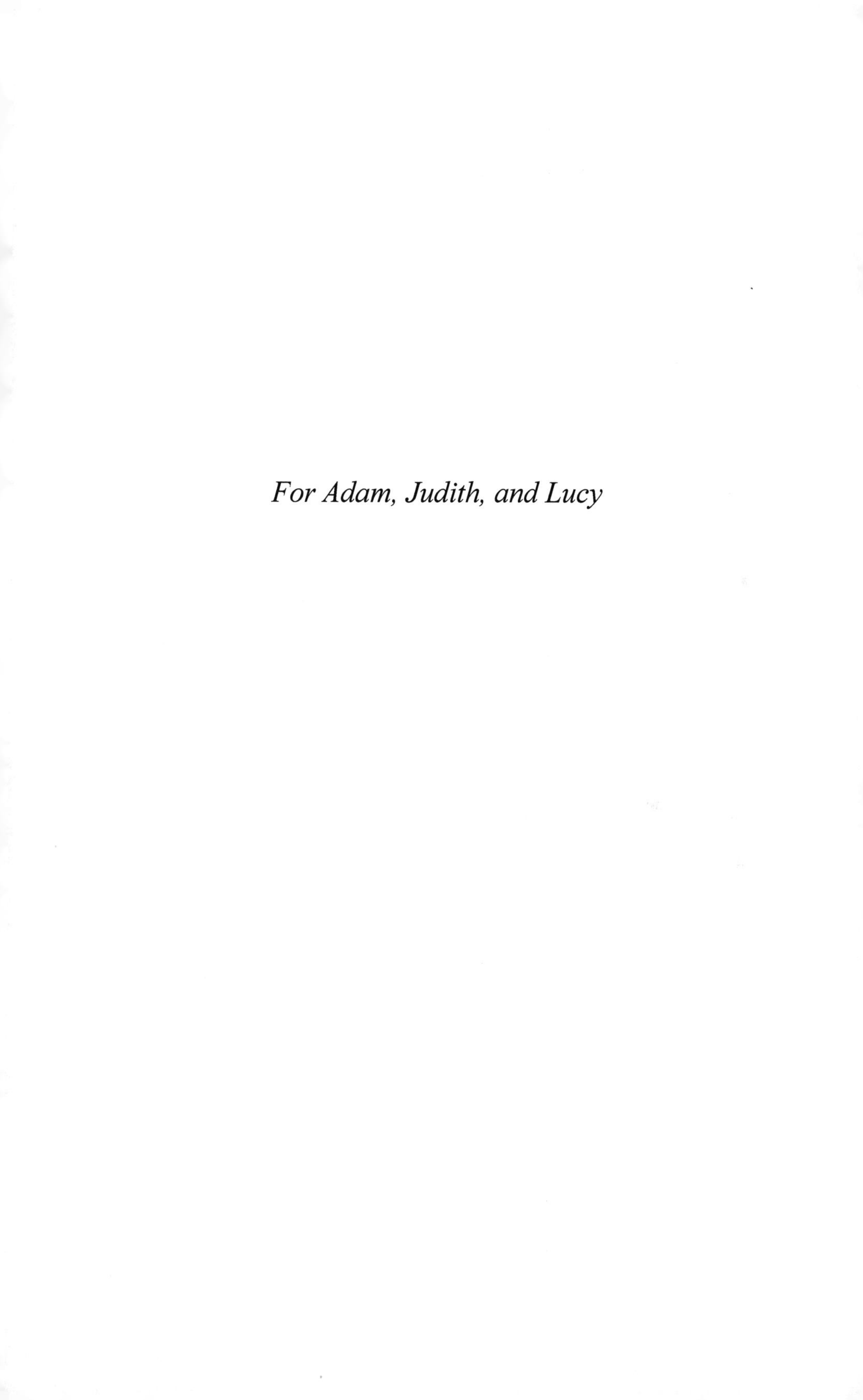

For Adam, Judith, and Lucy

With heartfelt thanks, yet again, to Marcelle Dubé and Keara Hlewka who helped produce this book

SARAH
A LOVE STORY

PREFACE

Sarah, my wife, was diagnosed with breast cancer in 1976. She had sixteen years clear of the disease, and as each year passed it seemed likely she was one of the lucky ones who had escaped its clutches. Then in April 1992 she felt discomfort in her chest wall that was shown to be due to spreading of the tumour in her bones.

The shock of this discovery was devastating for us both. Sarah set about dealing with it in her most pragmatic way – by reading all she could find about breast cancer, by using relaxation self-hypnosis, and exploring alternatives to conventional radiation and chemotherapy treatments, yet complying with the advice of her doctors at the Cancer Hospital.

Sarah slowed down little because of her illness. With her bold natural sense of colour she became a fanatical and skilful quilter. She travelled widely – twice to Britain alone to visit family and friends, thrice to the United States with me, and a couple of times across Canada as Yukon representative of the International Year of the Family. Then she began to feel pain in her hip where a fresh spot turned up on X-ray. "Oh, what a nuisance!" was her response.

In December 1993, a few days after returning from seeing her mother in England, she developed pain in her back and nerve symptoms in her legs that showed one of her spinal vertebrae had collapsed. Thinking that sunshine would do her good in the middle of a Yukon winter, in January 1994 we went on holiday to stay with a friend in San Miguel de Allende, Mexico. Despite her pain Sarah insisted on accompanying me round Central Mexico by train and bus on an adventure styled after the manner of several long overland journeys we had made abroad together in recent years.

In San Miguel we met Robert Philips, on holiday from his home on Hornby Island off the coast of Vancouver Island. Swiftly we formed a close friendship with Robert, who was a generation older than us. He had led a fascinating, peripatetic life, somewhat like our own. After a childhood in Brazil he went to school in England. In World War II he commanded a landing craft during the invasion of Italy. When a shell killed most of his boat's crew, he was posted to India. The war over, he rebuilt a derelict farmhouse for his family in North Wales. Then he moved to Canada where he became successful in the world of finance.

Robert retired early, along with his beloved wife Monica, to Hornby Island in an Arcadian setting of wild seas, rocky cliffs, and cedar forest. Then Monica developed Alzheimer's Disease, from which she slowly and remorselessly deteriorated. Robert nursed her at home until she finally had to enter a nursing home.

Sarah and I visited Robert's waterfront home on Hornby twice in 1994, enjoying his company and deepening our friendship. When Sarah's symptoms worsened I started writing letters to Robert telling him how she was doing, and how I was feeling about the whole sad situation that was full of anxiety and foreboding for both Sarah and me. I am usually rather a guarded fellow, but Robert had my total trust and I was able to pour out my concerns to him in these letters in a way I could not have done to anyone else.

I stored the letters away in my word processor and never looked at them again until after Sarah died, on 5 November 1995. Then I printed them out and read them to remind myself of the sad but happy roller coaster we had ridden together. The letters struck me as a tribute to a very courageous woman and, through them I wished to honour her despite the discomfort of opening my own soul on the way. Perhaps that in itself may encourage someone out there trying to support the person they most love, who is dying.

LETTER #1

WHITEHORSE, NOV. '94

Dear Robert,

Sarah and I spent a very happy month in Victoria, especially our visit to you on Hornby. We enjoyed goofing around, visiting friends, but most of all just being together. I treasure every moment in a heightened way since I have no idea how many moments are left. There's no one I'd prefer to spend long spells of time with than her, we so enjoy each other's company. We've been very lucky to share in our travels so much that is out of the ordinary. I'm sure you and Monica must have been the same, and that is why your own present pilgrimage with her illness is so cruel.

Recently I've been through some emotional stages that I'm sure you'll understand. At first when we knew Sarah's cancer had recurred I was devastated and just felt like crying all the time, partly for her knowing what was ahead and what she would have to suffer, partly for myself in selfish realization that I would before long be deprived of my *jiban sati* – as they say in Nepali – meaning my 'lifelong friend.' It's how I always think of her, lover though also she is. If I felt like this, I told myself, just imagine what she must be feeling. But I can't. She has to put up with the daily anxiety of living with a disease that is slowly eating her away, with pain that can only worsen, and with an uncertain future.

I got used to the idea that she was not going to die immediately, and for me the hurt became less acute. She needed all my empathy and understanding. Sometimes selfishly I have found this hard to give. She's the power of this pair, and I've found it really hard to be that strong one for a change. I listen to her troubles (which she vents so rarely) and yet I must not lean on her as I am used to do. Sometimes I want to tell her I've had a lousy day, or that I'm feeling low. Then I remind myself that my little worries are small fry compared to hers. I shut up and feel resentful, and despise my selfishness.

We seem to have settled into accepting this gremlin sitting on her shoulder. If he does not foul up her machinery at least we'll be prepared for him. She's getting quite a lot of pain from her spine, also from her hip. We know from her X-rays that she has lesions in both places. I just dread the day when these bones will collapse and fracture because of being weakened by the spreading metastases. Then she'll be in deep trouble. One of the problems of being in the medical business is that I know too darned much. I've seen it all before – but always it was someone else's problem, someone else's wife. Cancer never goes away, it just abates for a while but it usually comes back to haunt one. We've just been lucky to have seventeen free years – gratis you might say.

Anyway we still have a few good years together. First we plan to spend next spring in Europe, then if we can travel on the Trans-Siberian Railway, that'll be a bonus. It would be a nice way to round off our long overland journeys of the last few years.

Sarah's illness has made the future seem much more immediate, and I'm not obsessed with salting stuff away for our comfortable retirement. We live modestly and have ample. I've taken heed of what you said about preparing living wills and powers of attorney. I feel I can talk to her about it now, which I couldn't before – but in quite a detached way, as though we were always talking about some third party, not our very selves. Perhaps doing that will be a big relief for her because she's so much more pragmatic than me. We never talk about dying; it doesn't seem to be on her agenda yet. Perhaps it never will be.

You know, Robert, it's wonderful for me to be able to write all this to you. I could never be so frank with anyone else. I so appreciate your friendship, wisdom and empathy; no hidden meanings, no game playing. What I sees is what I gets, and I like it that way. It's the only way I know how to relate, and I haven't the patience to have it otherwise. Also it's the medical business again – you're not meant to have problems of your own when you spend all day dishing out potted wisdom like some oracle. When something like this hits you between the eyes it soon brings you to your knees.

Sarah has called a couple of times from England. She's having a good time in Suffolk with her mother who is a sharp and interesting lady, incredibly well-read and brimful of gossipy historical snippets. Sarah is going up to London tomorrow to spend time with her sister, Jean, near Hampton Court. Then she'll visit one of her friends in Bristol where we used to live before we came to Canada. I just hope she doesn't rush around too much because rest is so important for her. She'll be back a week tomorrow by when I'll have worked my way through all the President's Choice frozen dinners – cannelloni with three different cheeses, and two-cheese lasagna – so I never want to see pasta again.

To go back to our holiday, we had a very sociable time in Victoria where we have lots of Yukon friends. We were comfortable in our one-bedroom apartment on Penzance Street that we built in the basement of the house we bought when we moved down there five years ago –

supposedly permanently. We look out across the old Chinese cemetery to the sea where gigantic boats pass on their way to drop off the pilot before they head out down the Strait of Juan de Fuca to the Pacific. As you know, I only lasted six months living in Victoria. One wet, windy day as I cycled home I thought the tulips were shaking their heads and mocking me, and I couldn't stand the daffodils! So I turned and fled to our north country of the Yukon, while Sarah followed after she had finished her upholstery course.

Driving over the Coquihalla on the way to Kelowna the van gave a few coughs but settled down. In Banff Sarah insisted we stay in a motel, while I was quite ready to sleep in the van as it's so cozy. I put Sarah on the Calgary airport bus to fly to Montreal for a conference of the International Year of the Family of which she is the Yukon representative. There she spent time with our son, Adam, who is doing his Ph.D. Later she flew off to England – the gadabout! I then set off to drive the 2,500 kilometres back to Whitehorse in a spluttering van.

We've had lots of good snow and I have skied on our cross-country trails every day. I'm working on my stories (autobiography sounds so bombastic). At least it gets me into writing mode until I find the inspiration to start something more original. I once wrote an appalling novel about a crooked doctor on the Amazon, and I may try to revive it because the story itself is good.

Letter #2

Whitehorse, 5 Dec. '94

Dear Robert,

Sarah isn't well and I just wanted to write to you about her. She had a wonderful time in England, staying with her mother and visiting friends. The only thing that bothered her was her hip that has been sore for weeks now. We know she has three spreading lesions there, so pain is to be expected. On her return, apart from jet lag, she looked radiant.

Then she started to mention some pain radiating from her back to her shoulder blade. It got worse and settled in the centre of her back right over the vertebra where X-rays show a metastatic lesion. Now she's in bed and is only comfortable propped up with pillows. Even sitting up is very painful. I've known for a long time that a compression fracture of her vertebra might happen, but I've closed my mind to the thought of it.

One of my partners, an anaesthetist who specializes in pain management, came to see Sarah at home and put her on morphine in fairly large doses. The pain settled a bit, but morphine doesn't touch it if she is up because the weight of her body puts pressure on her spine. She's due to go down to Vancouver in a week anyway as she had put off having some more radiotherapy to her hip until after her visit to England.

I'm scared rigid for her, Robert. Does this mean she could become paralysed and be totally bedridden? I understand perfectly well how that could happen, and I can't bring myself to face the thought of it. Again, the only thing she's said about it is, "Oh, what a nuisance!"

At present she's on a pull-out couch on the floor of our living room. It's bright and airy with pictures and her quilted wall hangings right up to the ceiling. The woodstove stands opposite her. She's in the centre of things and can boss me about, stumbling and fumbling as I do in the kitchen. One way she can look into her sewing room, the other she sees who is coming in the front door, and even sees out to Grey Mountain when the weather is clement.

It's a blessing we live in this small house. My criterion for the right-sized house is one that when you plug in the vacuum the cord stretches to every corner of the house without having to move the plug. These 'tin' houses were made in the US of steel sections twelve feet long by one foot wide that interlock like Lego, hence their name, 'Steelox.' They were erected in the war for servicemen maintaining the Alaska Highway – ours definitely for 'other ranks.' Unfortunately they were designed for the tropics but were shipped north as an emergency, and the insulation in the walls is made of stuff like padded envelopes.

The house is very compact and everything Sarah needs is all around her. We could always put up a bed there permanently if it comes to it. I doubt if she'll ever be able to use the loft over my study where we usually sleep because it involves some quite athletic climbing to get in and out of bed. Of course I'm thinking the worst; but I must be practical, which is against my better inclinations.

Dear girl, we have so many journeys still to do. We want to go on the Trans-Siberian Railway together. And she wants to come out to Nepal next year because she has never seen the Everest region where so much of my life has been focused. Now she faces the prospect of being a permanent invalid. I may be prematurely gloomy, but being in the business I know too much for my own comfort.

In Vancouver next week she will have a CT scan that shows what is happening in her bony spine. Even if it does show progression of the disease, what can they do about it? Nothing much. Just offer all sorts of nasty treatments that may be worse than the disease she is contending with already. I probably won't go with her to Vancouver because she prefers to be alone when she goes to the cancer clinic. It isn't just that she's being unselfish and sparing my feelings, she really does prefer to manage this on her own as long as I'm there to support her when she comes home. She likes to know all the answers, and she questions her two doctors unmercifully for the exact picture of her disease. Luckily she has total confidence in them, solicitous and caring as they are.

Oh, dear Robert, I'm not being very strong about this. It's wonderful to be able to write to you because I don't know anyone else with whom I could be as open. We both feel lucky to have met you so recently and to have become such good friends. I don't want to burden you, but just telling you makes me feel better because I know how much you care for her.

Perhaps by the time I write next things will turn out not to have been as bad as I am positing now. Let's hope so. I'm also frightened because I don't have any religious faith, and it's a bit late to be making overtures to St Peter now. I don't know what happens after this is all over, but I'm sure there are many things – death being paramount – that we were not meant to understand on this earth. I can't really imagine life without her. We've done everything together, wandered the world, and have had thirty-four wonderful years in partnership.

Letter #3

Whitehorse, 20 Dec. '94

My dear Robert,

It was grand to hear you on the phone. Thank you so much for visiting Sarah in the Cancer Hospital. She said she returned to her bed and found you waiting, which cheered her no end. It's been a hellish two weeks, Robert, and I want to tell you about it. The therapy is in the writing the letters and knowing that you are reading them at the other end – and caring.

Let me go back to Monday two weeks ago. I told you Sarah had been having pain in her shoulder blade, but it got much worse and was centred over her T4/5 spine where we knew there was disease (also at T12). She had noticed some numbness in her feet, and difficulty in knowing when her bladder was full. Fortunately one of my partners recognized the neurological signs of spinal cord compression. He arranged for her to fly down to Vancouver immediately. I returned from skiing to find a message on our answering machine telling me to be ready in an hour to escort her down on the plane.

In Vancouver right away they realized Sarah was an acute emergency. They put her on big doses of steroids to try to lessen the swelling causing pressure round her spinal cord. Her two doctors took the trouble to explain everything and to answer all her questions, which makes her feel more in control. She's mighty nosey, as you know. An MRI scan showed that the disease has slowly extended into her spine. So she had nine short, sharp bursts of radiation aimed right at the lesions. This was enough to knock her socks off. Now they plan to give her chemotherapy after New Year to try to halt the systemic spread – not a happy prospect. The hospital staff obviously love her because she is brave and uncomplaining.

I hate hanging about in hospitals, being on the other side of the fence. Everyone is so bossy, so efficient, so clinical. What else should I expect? I found myself continually on the verge of tears, and would suddenly get a crack in my voice at the most inopportune times. I just wandered round Vancouver in a state of deep gloom, trying to gather my wits for the next time I visited, so I wouldn't appear as feeble as I was. Sarah suggested I return home before the weekend to keep things on a level for the kids, as she was due to be discharged early next week.

I wrote the enclosed piece (q.v. *Hugs*) when I got back home. It came straight from the heart, and Sarah really liked it. I sent it to Derek Cassels, editor of *The Medical Post*, who has become a good friend over the years when I've been writing for him, and he will publish it as an editorial.

I had the weekend on my own at home. For precious moments I could ski in the woods where it is utterly silent and still, apart from the squirrels dashing across the tracks and up into the trees. I could pretend that it was going to be alright with Sarah.

She came home on Wednesday. We are lucky to live in so tiny a house – cozy like yours on Hornby. I bought two new sets of fitted sheets, green and burgundy, and she sits propped up with lots of pillows, holding court. Even the mail lady broke off her walk to stop by for a confessional of all the traumas in *her* life. When visitors come I make myself scarce in my study, but I hear the gist of chat from next door. Sarah has the incredible ability to move the conversation away from herself and turn it to the woes the visitor has come to lament.

Sarah can get up to the bathroom, but she's pretty whacked after a few minutes and has to return to bed. That break gives me time to straighten the sheets, brush off the crumbs, fluff her pillows, and turn back the quilt under which she likes to lie by day. I give her tea and toast for breakfast (she's just developed a yen for crackers and Marmite); then she gets her own lunch, and I make a fine line in moist scrambled eggs for supper. I'm a useless cook, but I'm learning.

Our elder daughter, Judith, lives next door and pops in often. She runs a family day home out of her house, and the kids play in the whole of our fenced backyard. She runs a tight ship – as we sometimes hear through the party wall – but the kids love her, and we think they get a very good deal. Grandson Tim frequently drops in here with his miniature dachshund, Rosie, who immediately gives Sarah a good licking all over her face, especially behind the ears. She had dachshunds as a child so she's very indulgent. Tim gives Sarah enormous pleasure ("Oh! I do love that little boy") and they play together, or watch *The Lion King* for the umpteenth time, while Judith goes out skiing.

So everyone is gathered around her; she always likes being the centre of attention. For the time being, while she has to be confined to bed, the house is about as ideal as if it was architect-designed for her. Thankfully we don't live in a huge, multi-level house with stairs and separate rooms. I often think of your comfortable house on Hornby – unpretentious, but beautiful and practical.

All the kids will be here for Christmas. I wonder how many days it will be before they get up each other's noses. It'll be grand to see them. Adam comes from Montreal where he's finishing off (so he assures me – but he's been reassuring me for rather a long time now!) his Ph.D in computer mathematics at Concordia University. We talk at least once a week on the phone – a family ritual – always collect. You'd enjoy him, Robert, he has such a quirky sense of humour. He's very bright and disputatious – unlike his retiring father – so you'd have fun philosophizing with him.

Lucy and Alain, our friend-in-law, come home tomorrow. She has just won a Canada Cup race series and qualified for the Canadian team to compete at the World Nordic Ski Championships in Thunder Bay in March. We are very proud. She has established her place as Canada's #1 woman cross-country skier. Not bad considering only a month ago she had surgery to repair a torn tendon in her thumb, dislocated in a fall while training in Italy. It's been very painful skiing with her pole splinted in place and strapped to her hand. As she says, when the race is underway everything hurts so badly she doesn't notice the pain in her thumb.

Lucy is thinking of hanging in to compete in another Olympics (she was racing in the winter Olympic Games in Albertville in 1992) – she had decided to retire at the end of this year, but is having second thoughts. Why not? At 26 she's only just coming into her own at the sport. The cross-country skiers often don't peak until their early 30s, and so many of the women, especially the Russians, have babies which they leave at home with granny. Lucy has put off her schooling and career for so long, what matter if it's another few years? Skiing is a full-time job now – no more the *Chariots of Fire* dilettante stuff. Alain has a good position with the national team as waxing technician (he retired last year after three Olympics – one cycling and two cross-country skiing) so they travel together. They've got lots of savvy so they'll get by somehow. Sarah and I always say it's no use worrying about our kids. They will live their life as it comes along, as we've all had to do. Sometimes things work out well, sometimes not. Them's the breaks.

I've gone on far too long and your eyes are probably strained by now. Give our love to San Miguel. Caitlin Press in Prince George is going to publish my Atlin book under the title *Atlin's Gold.* There's still lots wrong with it, even after five years' work and three re-writes (as suggested to me by Jan Morris), but it's the best I can do. Some of it is well written. It's me, and that's how people will have to take it, warts and all. The focus of the theme is the cabin; we all fit in as peripheral players, radiating out from, but always returning to, the cabin.

I'll write again soon to keep you abreast of Sarah's news. Poor girl, she's been through hell with the pain, and then the misery of radiation. And now there's more to come with the prospect of chemotherapy and no guarantee she'll ever get out of that bloody bed on the floor. She remains eternally hopeful and is planning how we will travel round Europe by car in the spring.

HUGS

Touch them. Go on. I dare you, touch your patients. It's your job and don't let any Royal College smart-ass tell you otherwise. There are many times in practice when words have no place, and a hand on the shoulder, a hug, or even a kiss are the only appropriate way of communicating our deep caring for our patients. Depriving ourselves of this essential tool, that costs not a penny, diminishes our armamentarium in a job where we have few enough tools to work with – just a prescription pad and some human kindness.

Hippocrates didn't deny us the right to touch our patients with love – but we transgress the line between agape and eros at our peril. If you can't distinguish between the two, the kitchen's too hot, so get out of it into some closet where you don't need to feel for people.

We're a touchy-feely family, and thankfully touching comes easily, even with patients. When my wife and I went to the airport to see Rosemary off for her liver transplant, I kissed her goodbye – a kiss that told her I had cared deeply for her these past years. Now she was off on a dangerous road and we were with her. Words would have been clumsy and redundant. Now, six years later, on each anniversary, I keep a special kiss for her. At the end of every visit of Mrs D, aphasic from a stroke, I kissed her farewell – a parting greeting. When young Irene, who I have cared for over a couple of decades, returned from being donated a pair of lungs, I hugged and kissed her with joy in front of my colleagues.

I love words, but there are times they fail me and only a touch will speak the volumes I wish to say. If we believe all the commissions and the malpractice Cassandras, we'll stay a studied distance from our patients for fear of being sued.

When I'm sick I want a bold and competent doctor with courage to do what s/he knows is best for me. When I dislocate my shoulder on a mountainside I want a hefty dose of morphine – at least double what they say in the books – and I want a rescuer to do what Hippocrates said, and put his heel in my axilla and pull steadily on my wrist. I do not want a namby-pamby who needs an X-ray in case he nips my brachial plexus. I want to be able to climb down safely with one arm free, and avoid dying of exposure on the way. If you can't take the risks of being a Good Samaritan, then eschew it altogether.

My wife has cancer. At the Cancer Hospital she has two of the most caring doctors I've ever encountered. They sit on her bed, hold her hand, touch her arm, and explain in bare detail what is going on. Women are better than us tight-arsed men; generally they're nicer human beings – it's their lack of testosterone.

Would that I have been so empathetic over the years with my own patients. Words between my wife and me get lost in tears. She just wants me to be near when she feels sad, to hold her hand and to hug her, to put my arms around her in bed and to hold her close and tight. I'm all choked up over it. When people, out of heartfelt kindness, ask me how she's doing, I'm liable to dissolve in a puddle.

I don't want platitudes; I don't want a box of tissues. I just want someone to be bold and touch me, put a hand on my arm, give me a hug. Costs nothing, means millions.

Letter #4

Whitehorse, 25 Dec. '94

My dear Robert,

A few days ago when the kids returned it was -4C in bright sunshine – perfect for skiing. However, as always when Adam comes home, it dropped to -32C, which made for a pretty chilly ski this Xmas morning.

Adam is back from Montreal and staying next door with Judith. Lucy and Alain are sleeping in our spare loft in Sarah's sewing room along with all their ski gear packed for Europe. They don't travel light! So it's pretty crowded but is a very convivial gathering of the family, and Sarah loves having all the kids around her. It's amazing how they regress when they all come together, as if they each cut their age by half and return to their old teenage ways, niggling each other and vying for attention. Did yours do the same? I have to remind Sarah that even now sparks fly when she and her sister, Jean, are together, and they behave like a pair of rival teenagers.

Rob and Gai, friends of the kids (he was also my flying instructor), came over for a delicious ham dinner – a nice change from turkey. We watched slides of Sarah's and my shared journeys through China, Tibet, and India; the length of Africa from Nairobi to Cape Town and back; and to Antarctica and round Patagonia (three separate trips, not all at once). Lots of laughs and happy memories.

Sarah is utterly uncomplaining. She controls her pain with morphine, as long as she takes sufficient but not enough to space herself out. Of course she'd love to come off it because she knows she is becoming dependent – probably addicted too. For the moment she needs it, so what's the point of putting up with pain that just drains the spirit out of a person? She's so beautiful lying there it's hard to realize that inside a beastly monster is eating away at her. She thinks the spinal cord compression symptoms are subsiding and the numbness is less. Silly old bugger me, Worst-case-scenario Man, as she always calls me – perpetual optimist that she is. I wish I didn't have the inside knowledge of the medical business. Never mind, we must hope and plan because that gives her reason for living. We talk of going to Europe in spring. Perhaps that will be possible, but I'll have to put the Trans-Siberian on hold because I cannot leave her alone for a month.

Sarah is so loved, people coming to visit her often end up in floods of tears. She does that to people. She emanates strength and love and concern for others, and can turn a conversation away from herself in a trice. It knots me up inside that I'm not as strong or as selfless as she is. I try to ski every day because that gives me some time on my own. I need it as we're pretty on top of each other in our tiny tin house. I found myself getting unwarrantedly irritated last week because she would want something just when I had sat down and got my feet into the sleeping bag that is the only way I can keep warm under my desk. Then I got mad with myself because I have no right to be so selfish when it's not me who is suffering in this business. Thankfully I am only working a day and a half a week. This allows me time to be with her, which would be difficult if I was full-time. In January for a couple of weeks I am doing a locum in my clinic for the doctor who bought my practice. That will be a pleasant contact with the patients again – not too committing, nor arduous.

I felt good about that piece, 'Hugs,' that I sent you. It took a bit of courage to be so personal in public, but it was how I felt at the time, and the words just flowed into the paper without much forethought. I had a call from the editor saying it was one of my best pieces (I've written over 100 for him) and he was going to publish it immediately as an editorial. It always feels good when someone you respect appreciates your work.

I'm excited about *Atlin's Gold*. I've signed the contract with Caitlin Press who is aiming to publish it in the middle of next year.

Sarah's illness is hard on the kids, and I feel very proud of the way they are handling it. Judith, our middle one, has just finished a course on early childhood development, which seemed as concerned with building the self-esteem of the teacher as of the child. Why not? That is what a child is going to notice. Despite being quite beautiful, athletic, and a lovely person, as a teenager she always had a poor image of herself. She never got better than a 'Pass' at high school, and considered herself a dummy. Sarah always had confidence in her different abilities – cooking, caring for children, expressive writing. Judith is certainly dyslexic for figures. She nearly quit the course after the first evening when she found out that half the class had university degrees. Anyway, it took several long walks in the woods to persuade her to give the course another chance. She hung in, and by halfway she got 98% for her journal, and 94% for her presentation on children. She ended with an 'A' – something she'd never dreamed of before. It made an amazing difference to many facets of her life. We are so delighted since, of all the children, she has had to work the hardest to get results.

Adam is doing well in Montreal. He has oceans of ability, but he's quite idle and takes an age to get into gear. However, he has the easygoing personality and quirky sense of humour of his mother. Lucy, despite surgery on her thumb only a month ago, won all her races in Thunder Bay and has qualified for the World Championship team.

Christmas must be a sad time for you, Robert, thinking of Monica imprisoned in a mind you can't access in order to share all the wonderful memories of a lifetime of Christmases with her and your family. You set me a good example in how to cope with adversity. I just write anything that comes into my head to you; no other people, apart from Sarah, are privy to my rather locked-up life. I guess that's why I've managed to handle the knocks. I know it's not the best, but it seems to work for me.

Letter #5

Whitehorse, 4 Jan. '95

My dear Robert,

I hope you had a good Christmas, though it must be difficult down in sunny Mexico raising the snowy images we associate with winter up here. On my pin-board I have a photo I took of you by the lacework rocks on Hornby, so you are often in my thoughts.

We had one of our jolliest Christmases ever. Her Majesty was on the couch bed in the middle of the living room, lording – or ladying – it over all comers in her own peculiarly regal way. For a few hours of the day the low winter sun streams through the big south-facing windows lighting everything. The picture-covered walls are gay with the addition of Xmas cards from all over the world, strung on ribbons. The woodstove keeps us warm (except in my study where I sit in a sleeping bag because there's not much insulation between me and the outside).

The children all had breakfast at Judith's next door so I could tidy up the house and get Sarah organized with her bath, etc. Then they would all take off in different directions catching up with friends, or skiing. I had a couple of good outings with Adam, and two hours with Lucy on her last day at home when we skied the whole of the Long Valley Trail with the sun shining and hoar frost on the trees.

We all went up to David and Eva Howe's for Xmas dinner; they are long-time Yukon-English friends who live on the hill behind us. Among some recently acquired family heirloom furniture was a *chaise longue* on which we arranged Sarah, comfortably bolstered with cushions. Their vast Newfoundland puppy, Kilvert, behaved well apart from swishing some crystal wine glasses off the ormolu table with his tail, nosing me in the crotch with a swift upper-cut of his snout, and slobbering over the front of my pants so it looked as if I'd had an embarrassing accident. He endeared himself to grandson Tim, who is about the same size, and both spent most of the evening together under the dining room table. We had crackers and paper hats and lots of laughs, which are Sarah's best therapy.

On Boxing Day some of us went to Atlin. Lucy stayed behind to look after Sarah. She has been away in Europe all winter, and is soon off again till spring, so it was a chance for her to dote on her mother free from the eagle eyes of her siblings. Sarah got very sick from a delayed stomach upset caused by the radiation. She was miserable for a few days with repeated dry heaves and bilious vomiting. It has settled down a bit now with the help of a new anti-emetic drug. She postponed her chemotherapy because of the vomiting, so she will start next week. I'm afraid it will make her sick again.

The Atlin cabin was cozy once we thawed it out by lighting the barrel furnace in the basement and letting the huge logs roar. We went down to the Atlin Inn for supper while the heat seeped into the walls of the house. When we returned a couple of hours later it was toasty warm. I slept in my Everest sleeping bag out in the porch where fern patterns sparkled on the ice of the windows. Judith and Tim were in the bunkhouse room, with Adam in the upper bunk. Alain slept on the living room couch over the heating vent.

We all skied out to Noland Mine, just as we have done on many Xmases over the past 20 years. Atlin has so many memories of the kids' childhoods. It's interesting to see how proprietorial they are about the cabin now, having for many years not wanted to go down there because it wasn't 'cool.' We all felt sad Sarah couldn't be with us to share the fun, but the journey would have been too long and tiring for her, and the biffy a problem.

(Back in Whitehorse), later 8 Jan. '95

Now the kids have all gone their several ways and it's very quiet round here. Sarah misses them as she just loved having them around her bed, and their continual coming and going. Adam has gone back to Montreal to work to finish off his Ph.D; it has been quite difficult for him because his supervising professor has gone home to Japan – perhaps permanently. Lucy and Alain flew to Sweden to pick up a van, rented by the national team, and drive it across the Norwegian border where they are having a high altitude training camp. The first World Cup race is in the Czech Republic, where I have a friend, Vladimir, who wants to show them round Prague. He got badly frostbitten doing a winter climb of Mt Steele (no relation) in the St Elias Range. Sarah nursed him and his companion, Ivan, on the floor of our living room to avoid them having to go into hospital. Since then I have seen him twice in Prague when I was there doctoring the Canadian ski team. Afterwards Lucy and Alain will return to Norway for a World Cup, and then back to Canada to train for the World Championships in Thunder Bay in early March. I'm planning to go down to watch; I've never seen her in a major race because she abhors having her parents hanging around, but now I think she really wants me there. Sarah is fiercely proud of her and would love to be there to cheer her on.

So we try to carry on as normal, Robert, but Sarah gets quite discouraged by her lack of progress, especially when she's feeling sick from the chemo, and from the morphine that she monitors herself. I'm more on an even keel now and not as weepy as I was, although it sometimes strikes me at the most inappropriate moments. Writing to you lets it all hang out; I just hope I don't bore you. This machine lets me pour out the words at speed, such as I could never do in longhand. Hence the verbal torrent that doesn't lead to better writing.

LETTER #6

WHITEHORSE, 9 JAN. '95

My dear Robert – my friend and sounding board,

Sarah was doing fine. The pain in her back had eased enough to allow her to stop taking morphine. Her stomach was beginning to settle after the upset caused by the radiation. The nausea, vomiting, and dry heaves that have plagued her for a week began to subside. She had a miserable time escaping from the clutches of Morpheus, which made her shaky and irritable for a couple of days – all symptoms she understood well from her job as a drug and alcohol counsellor. She seemed to be on an upward course and would be well enough next week to start chemo, having postponed it to let her get back on her feet again.

Then in the middle of the night she called me into the bathroom to see her leg that was red, mottled, swollen, and painful. I knew immediately that it was probably the clotting of a deep vein, but tried to persuade myself to the contrary, hoping it might only be a superficial inflammation. I didn't want to disturb her doctor in the night, so we waited till morning. (I remember, when Adam had whooping cough as a kid, waiting till after 8 a.m. before we dared phone the doctor!)

I called Ken Quong, the young physician in our practice, who takes care of Sarah. He came to see her at home. Because of the swelling up her thigh he was confident that it was a clotted deep vein, so decided she should be in hospital for anticoagulant treatment. The problem with deep vein thrombosis is that the clot may break off and send it into the lungs, which can be life-threatening. Because her leg was so painful she didn't put up much resistance to going into hospital.

Now the poor girl is fighting to get ahead. As soon as she takes one step forward she slides two backwards. God, it hurts to watch her, and to know the despair that must be going through her mind. She's wondering whether she can tolerate chemo at all, and whether it will do her any good. All I can do is hug her and tell her how much I love her. Oh! Robert, it hurts, and I'm numb from the crown of my head to the soles of my feet. I haven't cried for days, which worries me. It's like a bad dream where I'm standing on the outside watching this drama unfold without any control of the situation, and powerless to really help her.

The house is empty and I'm feeling sorry for myself. I've made up her bed as usual in the living room and it's empty. I'll probably sleep in it tonight just because I can't stand seeing it there without her in it. I want to have a jolly good cry, but somehow I can't. Judith shmucked her new car this afternoon, driving into someone who pulled over suddenly to pick up a hitch-hiker – a friend of ours, as it happens. She was probably concentrating on her worries about Sarah, rather than on the road. She was understandably upset; she doesn't need that sort of problem at this juncture.

Now that I've spilled the beans I feel better. I'll go and tuck up on Sarah's couch and re-read James (Jan) Morris's *Imperial Trilogy* which should keep me occupied for most of the winter, it's such readable history. Good night, dear friend, I'll talk to you in a day or so.

11 JAN. '95

Sarah is much better today but she's still in hospital. Her leg is less swollen and she's been getting a new, vastly expensive anti-nausea drug. She's much relieved and has decided to go ahead with chemo this Thursday. It will be good for her to have the first one in hospital in case she gets sick, but then I want to get her home as soon as she is able. The nurses are very solicitous, but I hate seeing her in that coldly clinical bed. I perch on the commode beside her – you mustn't sit on the bed because it crumples the covers – and we talk. But it's not like home. Besides, the old lady with the bowel problem in the bed next to Sarah keeps farting thunderously, which interrupts our conversation.

Sarah has more visitors than she wants or needs. Of course, the doctors ignore the 'No visitors' sign on the door, and just barge in presuming she'll be pleased to see them. Then they stand at the foot of her bed and pour out their problems. One stayed for 45 minutes, which exhausted her. I've told her she should charge a counselling fee.

I'm feeling more together today. Yesterday I was uptight all day, afraid I would burst into tears if someone spoke harshly, or kindly, to me. It all seemed so unfair that she's had to battle for twenty years this monster that has cast a shadow on our lives. The anxiety eased in the middle as she got more and more years clear of the diagnosis. By five years we thought she might be cured; by ten we were sure she was; by fifteen we'd almost put it out of our minds – then, whammo! I'm sure she'll get over this blip and go on for more years. Every day is precious now, and we want to live them to their fullest. There's so much we want to do together yet.

New snow fell last night so I went for a ski today. The trees were utterly beautiful mantled with fluffy snow, the swish of skis in new tracks and the crunch of poles biting the snow made me feel much better. I really do need those silent moments on my own in the woods to get it all together. Then I come back feeling human again.

These letters are a selfish form of indulgence written to a true friend. I get enormous support by just knowing you are out there caring. Please don't ever think you have to reply. There's nothing really to say. You say it all with your love.

LETTER #7

WHITEHORSE, 18 JAN. '95

My dear Robert,

Sarah is back from hospital ensconced in her throne-bed on the floor. Today we received a lovely card from you, which was a joy. We hope you are all having a good winter down in the balmy clime of San Miguel. It has warmed up to spring-like -12C here. A friend from Victoria sent up to Sarah some snowdrops. They were beautiful, but just rubbed in how long we have to wait until the first crocus (Pasque Flower) will appear on the banks of the esker by the airport. The spring sun melts the snow there some time in April.

Sarah is still in quite a lot of pain from her very swollen leg, but the pain in her spine seems to have subsided, or is better controlled by her bumping up the dose of morphine. The two home nurses, Gail and Pat, call in most days so I take no part in her drug regime. They check that she is taking the right dose, but she prefers to manage it entirely by herself. She is taking anticoagulant rat poison by mouth and, apart from a mass of bruises from the intravenous, she's looking fine and is delighted to be home again. So we just have to get over this hurdle and then she'll be up and running – metaphorically. People have been very kind dropping round with soups and lasagnes and so on; they must know what a useless housekeeper I am. There's a great outpouring of love towards Sarah, which is very sustaining, but hardly surprising since she's the most universally loved person I know.

This note is just a quickie to let you know that things are improving, because I must have appeared so bloody miserable in my recent letters. I'm working again full time this week for my colleague. It's been fun being back at the clinic and not having to worry about the long-term responsibility for the patients. I'm longing to get back to my own story. I am having such fun researching and writing it.

LETTER #8

WHITEHORSE, 3 FEB. '95

My dear Robert,

Thank you so much for your letter; Sarah was delighted with yours to her, which arrived today. She is on the upward swing and is looking and feeling much better. She has started reading for the first time in a month, and is planning a new quilting project. She's getting very bossy, queening it over me in my own kitchen, so I *know* she's better. It has been just one thing after another, any one of which would have been enough to lay a normal person low. And she developed a tooth abscess, which was the last straw because pus lurking around makes anyone feel lousy. With her immune system buggered up by the radiation and chemotherapy she doesn't have enough white cells to combat the infection.

I try to insist that she comes out for a drive every day, so we are getting to know the back alleys of Whitehorse very well. If things go on improving like this we might get down to Atlin for a night next week. She finds she needs to top up her morphine before she goes out, and then it will last her for the trip; otherwise the pain in her back is just too much to be able to enjoy the outing. We may well make it to Victoria in April, in which case we'll visit Hornby. If things go well we could even get over to Europe to do part of our original spring plan. I'm quite content to live day by day and just see how things work out. Every day is precious now and we have to use each one to its fullest.

Dear Robert, you've been so good at listening to my wailing. It's very therapeutic, even if self-indulgent, to write to someone who really cares. I'm so much better at expressing myself on paper than I am in talking.

I'm glad you had a good time at San Miguel. It's nice for us to be able to imagine where you are and what you are doing. It sounds as if Fen's painting is going well. I covet the one at the top of her stairs, of some bucks eating from the lower branches of a tree – all in yellows. Has she forgiven us yet for not answering the phone that day when we were talking up a storm?

The days are lengthening noticeably. I don't have to hurry out to ski at midday because it's still light at 5.30 p.m. I do all my thinking out on the ski trail and it's as close to meditation, or prayer – call it what you will – of which I am capable. I just swish along in rhythm with my mind detached from my body, and thoughts race through my brain. Out there in the forest is where God resides, in every tree (are they the souls of those who have gone before?), in the squirrels that run across my path, and in the moonlight and the stars when I go out to ski at night. S/he is all around and in everything that has life. I'm working hard to get away from the concept, so bred into us, of the father figure up there in the clouds. I guess heaven is really this great world that we are in for the moment, and which we have moulded in ever so tiny ways to change and, we hope, to make it better for our passing.

I'm not a philosopher as you are, Robert. I just fly by the seat of my pants and hope it will turn out right in the end. I do know I have little time for the formal religions and all their intolerances. The bible is great as literature, and there are some fine stories in among the blood and guts, hellfire and brimstone. I don't know how anyone could believe most of that garbage, other than as legend. Actually I do know because in my youth I went through a religious spell that I see now as a huge, brainwashing con-trick. Many things we were never meant to understand, foremost of which is what's beyond the Great Beyond.

You will be back on Hornby soon, so that's where I'll send this letter. Once I sit down at this machine it's so easy to churn out the words compared to writing by hand. That's why handwritten letters are usually better. But for the purpose of letting it all hang out this machine is probably best.

LETTER #9

WHITEHORSE, 19 FEB. '95

My dear Robert,

It was good to hear your voice on the phone and to know that you had such a good time in Mexico. I wish I could have had time to whip up to Hornby to see you, but my time in Victoria was very short.

Sarah is generally a little better. She waxes and wanes, even over the course of a day. I tell her that when she's been so ill, not with one illness but with blow after blow, it would knock the stuffing out of any healthy person. She dreads chemo the most, but so far it has only made her a little nauseated. We hope she will improve enough for us to get down to Victoria for a visit at the end of April because blossoms should be out down your way then. May is a 'nothing-month' up here – the snow is dirty but hasn't gone, skiing is over, and few flowers are out yet. At the moment she can last about a couple of hours up and about, then she has to go back to bed because the pain in her back troubles her so.

I was on a course in Victoria run by the hospice people: *Dealing with Death.* I told Sarah I was doing a general practice refresher course because I didn't have the courage to tell her what it was really about. That wouldn't make you proud of me, Robert, would it? I guess I should have discussed it with her, but I can't talk with her about death – *her* death. I think I'm waiting for her to open the subject, and she's probably waiting for me to do the same. It will happen when the time is right and we are ready to do so. Robert Buckman, the radio and TV doc, was talking – extremely well. We both used to write for *World Medicine*, a magazine in the UK. The course was helpful for me if only to realize that we are just at the beginning of a long and painful journey. It gave some suggestions on how to cope with the suffering of someone you love. I have an unjustified suspicion of hospice. Sarah was visited by one of the newly formed Whitehorse group and she felt they were, at best, like beginners needing practice, at worst vultures hovering.

Being constantly on duty with someone who is very ill (as you well know) is very draining, and we've still got a long road to go. Lucy has been at home to watch Sarah so I was glad for the break. I'm soon going down to watch her ski in the World Championships – one proud dad!

I've just heard from the Caitlin Press who want my final edited *Atlin's Gold* by the middle of next month. Every time I look at it I become more aware of its failings, so I'm inclined to let it lie. Their editor, a beat-up old ex-schoolmaster with nicotine everywhere, seems to be quite competent, so I await his suggestions. I just hope he's gentle with my baby.

LETTER #10

WHITEHORSE, 27 FEB.'95

My dear Robert,

Your wonderful letter arrived a couple of days ago and had Sarah and me in stitches. We could just see you sitting swearing at the computer and tearing your hair out as text vanished into thin air.

Sarah is *much* better. She's still in bed most of the time, but we get out for a drive every day. She's been out alone to visit friends, and recently we went to a concert together. For some of these outings we are resigned to using a wheelchair – quite a step as it feels like defeat to her – but it makes moving about much easier. A couple of hours are about her limit, which gets longer all the time. We're going to drive to Atlin tomorrow for the night. A friend, Wayne Merry, who lives down there, will light the fire, so by the time we arrive the cabin will have absorbed the heat into the walls, and should be toasty warm. We've booked to come to Victoria for two weeks from 12-24 April, so if all goes well we'll come up to Hornby for a couple of nights. Please do *not* change anything around for us. It will be marvellous to see you again.

I'm busy writing my story (as I call it) and it's going quite well – I think! The telling will be when I get up the courage to ask you to read a draft for me; but that won't be for a few months. I've no idea whether the story will interest anyone else. It doesn't have the drama of your wartime adventures. The only thing I can do is to bash away, write the best English I am able, and see what turns up in the end. If I worry about a potential audience now, I'd never keep going.

It's been cold but sunny, and the skiing is grand – my secret weapon. Snow is on the trees, and all the world in my forest is clean and white. The sun rises higher in the sky now, and there's some heat in it; so even at 20 below in the morning it has warmed up a lot by midday. Aspens make long shadows on the snow, and pussy willow buds are appearing. I swish through the woods following in the steps of my girls, who both ski like angels. I competed a lot at Masters level until my hips started becoming arthritic. In a strange way I was glad because it slowed me down and broke my obsession with competing. Lucy called last night to say she had just won this year's Canada Cup after her races at 100 Mile House.

Today, for a change, I went for a walk in the woods from our front door, past Paddy's Pond, on a route Judith and I usually take in summer. Squirrels are everywhere, and there are spoor of snowshoe hares. We've seen a few robins that tell us spring is just round the corner. It will do Sarah so much good to be able to have the front door open and to look outside from her bed. When we go out for our drives she often says to me, "We couldn't have found a more beautiful place to live, could we?"

I've been doing an excellent Spanish course on Knowledge Network TV. I'm reading *Como Agua para Chocolate* in Spanish with the help of the dictionary and an English translation that I use to check each paragraph. Now I need the excuse to speak the language. We have a good friend who has just bought a farm up in the cloud forest of Costa

Rica, and he's trying to persuade Sarah and me to visit him next winter. Very tempting. Meanwhile she tolerates me mumbling Spanish at the TV every Tuesday evening. She's not too hot at languages, but every now and again she blurts out something startling.

So, dear Robert, take care. You'll probably not hear from me for a few weeks because I leave on 8 March for a few days in Toronto to visit my Tibetan lama friend; then on to Thunder Bay.

LETTER #11

WHITEHORSE, 19 MAR.'95

My dear Robert,

Your letter awaited me on return from Thunder Bay. You sound in good heart, even if your sight is a bit wobbly. Be reassured that the advice you've had from the Eye Care Centre is the best available.

Sarah improves daily. She looks awfully frail, and she can only stand in the kitchen for about 20 minutes; however, each day is a step forward. We go out for a daily drive and, now that the days are warming up, she will soon be able to sit out on the front step. Snow still covers the lawn. She remains constantly positive, and we are so looking forward to coming down to Victoria. Each of these little achievements is a great stride for her and, who knows, we may make it to Britain in the fall. I doubt if we'll be up to touring our friends in Europe as planned. She loves to visit her mother, of whom she is deeply fond.

I had a good time on my trip down east (Newfies always 'go down north on the Labrador, bye'; and 'up south to Saint Jaaahn's'). I went to see my dear friend Lama Sonam Tobgyel Rinpoche from whom I took Tibetan lessons when he was living in the Yukon. As he spoke no English, and I no Tibetan, we had to conduct the lessons in Nepali at which we are both reasonably fluent. He is patently a spiritual man and yet full of fun. We share many acquaintances along the length of the Himalaya, and he wants me to make a pilgrimage with him to visit his monastery in Tibet where he was discovered as an incarnate lama. Tempting, eh?

Lucy was delighted that I came to watch her at the World Championships in Thunder Bay. I positioned myself on the course so, by jumping a few snow-fences, I could get close to her at three or four different places on the course. I yelled till I was hoarse, and waved a huge Canadian flag. Afterwards she told me she could remember each time she passed me. Cheers mean a lot when you are flogging your guts out. I was mighty proud of her competing against the world's best. Now she has announced that she and Alain want to get married in Atlin in July! Adam may follow suit in September.

When I got home Sarah gave me a race-by-race account of Lucy and we watched on TV her final one that I had missed to get back to my eye clinic. We were both choked up with pride and tears rolled down our cheeks. Sarah has done remarkably well while I was away, with the help of Judith and lots of friends calling by, so I feel almost redundant!

Letter #12

Atlin, 1 Apr. '95

My dear friend Robert,

It's hard to believe that we may be visiting you within a couple of weeks DV (whoever D is, I just hope s/he is *volente*). I've had a lousy 'flu for about two days – sore throat, aches in all my limbs and back, no appetite, uninterested in reading, lying in my bed all day like a 'wet fallen leaf' (the sobriquet Japanese men give their fellows who help their wives in the house; as opposed to 'cockroach husband,' which applies to a younger man who is helpful in the kitchen). As I lay there feeling sorry for myself, and trying to keep clear of Sarah so hopefully she wouldn't catch it, I thought: 'this is how Sarah feels *every day*, and for her there's no end in sight.' What an amazing lady! She never complains, yet I know her back is hurting most of the time. For months she hasn't felt up to reading or quilting, which is her passion; and for most of the day she's confined on her back like Kafka's *Gregor Samsa*. So I quickly stopped bemoaning my ill fortune.

Despite it all, Sarah has made considerable strides in the past month.

She has driven herself downtown a couple of times – but she returns whacked out. She has been doing a little in the kitchen; though after about 20 minutes she has to lie down. And we are excitedly planning our trip to Victoria. I think every step is a giant leap forward for her, and so we take it easy – one day at a time. When we come to you please don't make any special arrangements. The studio room will be just fine. I don't want you turning the house on end for us.

I'm down in Atlin just for the night, with our friend-in-law, Alain, whom we love dearly. I'm sitting at the stout fir table, which I built twenty years ago, surrounded by all the knick-knacks we love. The cabin has become the haven for all the bits & pieces we couldn't hang in our refined slum in Tin Town (Hillcrest) Whitehorse – some of Sarah's early appliqué pictures; my photo of a coy Sherpa girl in Namche Bazaar; an old oven door that Sarah's father hauled out of a hedgerow in Wales and scrubbed clean until Queen Caroline's head with three plumes showed through; the old Jubilee woodstove borrowed from John Harvey, who mined on McKee Creek.

This little house has become the repository of so many of our family dreams and memories – a veritable treasure trove. And that's what my book, *Atlin's Gold*, is all about. It's not about the family *per se*, but about us radiating out from this very building, which has a life of its own. It's like a dear old family pet – cat Maude a decade ago, now Victor – always there to listen when you want to talk, never answering back harshly. The cabin is warm within a few minutes of lighting the fire, and retains its warmth as if it had never been left to freeze solid in mid-winter. When Sarah and I have been on journeys and the going got rough, it was always to the cabin that our thoughts returned. We could picture its blue shiplap walls, its gabled front porch, and windows with white trim like a friendly face.

Isn't it strange, looking back at events that made fundamental crossroads in our lives? Often we don't recognize their importance at the time, nor do we foresee the benefits of a certain move. A decision may appear disastrous then yet correct in retrospect. Which only goes to show that there's no way we can plan for this funny old passage of ours – called *Life* – we just have to get on and live it fully day by day, minute by minute. I guess Sarah's illness has brought all this into focus. I'm as happy now, surrounded by her ill-health – sadness, fear, gloom, pain – as I have been for ages. It's her and me in this together.

Why did we come to Canada in the first place – perhaps the most drastic decision we ever took, made one morning at breakfast? Unable to cope with the surgical rat race in Britain, I could see I wasn't going to make it as a surgeon. That was a terrible pill to swallow, as I have a fine pair of hands like my father. I fucked it up by going off to Bhutan, and Everest, and legions of other distracting sorties that made my CV look like a travel agent's itinerary. If I'd stayed in surgery I'd have got the egocentric disease that most of them get who have spent too much time under the spotlights, centre stage in the operating theatre.

So we came to Canada. Our kids abrogated a tidy grammar school (or worse, private school) with cricket, racquets and squash, and 'wilderness holidays' in mid-Wales. Before we left I burned my grandfather's moth-eaten Black Watch kilt – a symbolic gesture of starting afresh in the New World. The kids have never let me forget it. The sporran, said by grandfather to have been picked up at Culloden, looked like road-kill. It was a gesture to myself of leaving all that behind (I ditched my tails suit and grey top hat too) and making a new start.

We've never regretted the move. It was difficult for several years accustoming myself to not being a surgeon. I was a kindly GP, probably more interested in skiing than in aches and pains, but fine when someone had a real problem, or an emergency. Together Sarah and I built a good home. Most of the credit goes to her for that – utterly unperturbed in a storm, generous to drive me to distraction, patient when I wanted action. We delight in our kids and watch their progress with pleasure. I don't envy them having to make their way in a world through which I sailed with ease. As we say to ourselves, 'We must not allow their problems to vex us; they've got to live their own lives in their own way.' We try to appreciate their difficulties and support them, but we can't cushion them entirely from slings and arrows.

LETTER #13

VICTORIA, 19 APR. '95

My dear Robert,

What a wonderful visit! Whenever we leave Hornby, Sarah and I spend the next hour or two (and several days as well) rejoicing in our good fortune at having such a friend. Thank you for making her so comfortable. We would like to have stayed longer, but even that journey was a big step forward for her – the longest trip she has made for several months. It did her morale so much good, and we're even planning trips for the fall – possibly to Ireland – after we've visited her mother in Suffolk.

As we left Hornby, Sarah said, "One day I'd like to have one of Fen's paintings." I'm longing to see her face when she opens the parcel so carefully packaged by the little elf at the gallery round the corner from you. It will be a twofold joy. One, that we have a 'Fen'; the other that the *Denman Lighthouse* will constantly remind us of your beautiful homestead. The lighthouse draws the eye from wherever one is on your land, or in your house.

Robert, you have the uncanny ability to make everyone you touch feel they count. Your mind is supple, unfixed in its views, receptive of ideas. No wonder you have such a galaxy of friends. We had so many interesting talks with you. The deep philosophical stuff is lost on me – I must be a very shallow fellow.

I know what I don't believe in but I'm not so sure what I do. What does it matter because none of us knows the answers? Whatever you believe in, it's just speculation anyway. The important thing seems to be to get on with the living side of it (as you have done in full measure), and all will be revealed in its own good time. So long as we've done the best job we can along the way, and not hurt anyone in the process, then we should have nothing to fear. It's a wonderful world for the most part, despite it's peopled by a few lousy human beings among mostly mighty fine ones.

When I return home I'll send you instalments of my 'story' that I've been working on. Please scribble comments in the margin. Writing it has been a cleansing process, reliving things in detail that might otherwise have gone up in a puff of smoke, never to be recalled. Besides which, it gives me something tangible to get my writing teeth into. I haven't the imagination to be a novelist, but I can describe things I've seen or done. I can't imagine your grief, when your studio burned down, at losing the manuscript of your North Wales story and other wartime events and adventures.

VICTORIA, 20 APR. '95

This is going to be one of those narrative letters because I can't print it until I get home to Whitehorse. In Victoria all the blossom is out, and the rhododendrons and azaleas are in full bloom. We took Ted and Nicky Harrison to the University Garden (much smaller but lovelier than the Butchart Gardens). Julie Cruickshank and Caroline Kennard joined us and pushed Sarah round in her wheelchair in warm sunshine. She was utterly content. Ted rounded off a happy outing by reciting *Albert and the Lion* and its sequel as we sat on a bench outside the Inter-Faith Chapel. As a boy Ted used to do these recitations travelling round working men's clubs in the north of England.

As I sit at my desk in our little basement apartment I can look out through the garage doors, across Penzance St to the Chinese cemetery. Heavy tanker traffic is passing through the Strait of Juan de Fuca, and some sailboats are heading for the short cut to Oak Bay inside of Trial Island. In the far distance are the smoke stacks of Port Angeles and the snow-covered Olympic Mountains, with Hurricane Ridge very distinct in the middle. If I walk out onto the rocks I can see the snow-capped volcanic cone of Mount Baker. We are very lucky to have this place, and hope our tenant upstairs will stay.

Sarah has her appointment at the Cancer Hospital with Dr Susan O'Reilly as we pass through Vancouver. I found a postcard in her book with her prepared questions. It read:

- Haemoglobin 8.8 What do you recommend? Blood transfusion. Iron.
- How much improvement on back X-rays.
- Should I stop after 7th chemo. May 19th. a month before wedding
- Is there any point starting late?
- If I need radiation for pain control I can come down in June after wedding
- ?Start taking Megace drug?

That shows how much control she likes to maintain. I don't envy her doctors. We usually like nice quiet, compliant patients who don't challenge us with questions. Both Susan O'Reilly and Charmaine Kim-Sing, Sarah's radiotherapist physician, are utterly frank with her, yet gracious and caring.

We've had a pretty social time in Victoria and Sarah has done mighty well, but I have to watch that she doesn't get too tired. I remind her that since November, up until two weeks ago, she hasn't been out of bed for more than a couple of hours at a stretch. This morning we both agreed we were ready to head home to the Yukon, much though we've enjoyed being here. We just lock up the apartment and walk away from it – until next time.

BACK IN WHITEHORSE, 25 APR. '95

Home again, home again! The snow is off the lawn, but it's still on the trails in the woods. Judith and I have just done our walk that starts directly across the road, goes into the forest, and makes a big circle of Paddy's Pond on bush trails. It takes about an hour to complete. Our walks are very special times for us to talk. Judith and I communicate best when we walk, hike, or ski together. We don't seem to have had much chance recently because she has been very busy with her day home. I'll have to get in shape for our hiking season because trying to keep up with the bunch of athletes in our family is pretty hard work for an old fart.

I'm going to close this letter now or, trying to answer yours, I might be tempted to philosophize – and you know I'm hopeless at that. I'll think up something terribly profound with which to strike you dumb in my next letter.

Letter #14

Whitehorse, 22 May '95

My dear Robert,

You should have seen Sarah's face when she saw Fen's painting of the Denman Island lighthouse. We were just waiting for the start of a small party to celebrate our wedding anniversary (34 years) and several birthdays all occurring around the same time (my 60th). I sent Sarah next door to see the cake Judith had baked for us. I stayed behind and rearranged the pictures, putting Fen's right where she could see it from her bed in the middle of the living room. Sarah erupted in joy to be reminded of Fen and of you at one fell stroke (or several of the brush). Above it stands a pencil drawing of a sleeping cat by Lilias Farley, a patient of mine who was a pupil of Varley (Group of Seven) at the Vancouver School of Art; below is a painting of two Iraqi children done on a Marks & Spencer cardboard shirt stiffener by a surgeon from Baghdad who trained with me in plastic surgery at Bristol; to the right stands the big blue painting of superimposed horsemen and motor-bikers, *Urban Cowboys,* of a Bristol art teacher friend.

Thank you so much for your letter, it was good to hear from you. We've been enjoying the most amazing spring – often during the past month we were the hottest place in Canada. Sarah has been down to Atlin several times. The two-hour journey is tiring for her, but Atlin is restful as she so loves the place. She's fine when resting lying down, or sitting reclining, because the strain is off her diseased vertebrae. She can only manage a quarter of an hour or so vertical, then her back gets very uncomfortable. She tops up with morphine if she's going to be up for longer. She's on her one-from-last chemo, which is done at the hospital by a specially trained nurse in a quiet room with a reclining chair, so she can sleep if she wishes. Chemo always makes her feel pretty bloody, but she is as stoical as ever and never complains. Despite it all she looks wonderful – which is a bit deceiving.

We've just read *The River Sutra* by Gita Mehta, which is quite lovely and has some of the flavour of Rumer Godden's *The River*. We've also been absorbed with Harold Nicolson's *Portrait of a Marriage*. That pair ran a successful marriage with utter devotion despite Vita Sackville-West was having passionate affairs with Violet Trefussis and Virginia Woolf, while Harold was off with the boys. Then Vita and Harold would meet at weekends to plan the garden at Sissinghurst together. What a strange, eccentric, unconventional bunch were the Bloomsbury crowd.

I had a funny experience the other day. I was thinking of the piece I'd been writing about while walking from our Paddington flat through Hyde Park to St George's Hospital. I often saw the Household Cavalry riding across the bridge over the Serpentine with helmet plumes bobbing over their capes – but were the Horse Guards' capes blue and the Life Guards scarlet, or the other way round? Anyway, walking past the Whitehorse Public Library who should I see but Alan Byrom, once a Horse Guard himself, who used to work with Sarah at the Detox Clinic. In the middle of one night on duty he told her how he

LETTER #15

WHITEHORSE, 21 JUNE '95 – SOLSTICE

My dear Robert,

Many thanks for your lovely letter of 9 June. How well we know the feeling you describe so eloquently, of "…people breezing in for a little unannounced visit as though one is on holiday with nothing to do but sit on the porch bread-and-cheesing." We've been a captive audience so often that now I'm quite ruthless and have no conscience about telling them I'm busy and have work to do. The way you describe Hornby could easily be Atlin – people so laid back they are likely to fall over. Sarah and I have always taken the view, regarding visitors, that "What goes around, comes around." We've had so much hospitality from people on our travels abroad, we could never repay it other than vicariously to some unknown vagrant who turns up on our doorstep. We take the distant view that we may be entertaining angels unawares. Sometimes when they come out of the bush they smell less than angelic.

I enclose a photo of our living room with Fen's picture in place. You must be pleased she's coming to Hornby later in the summer (mid-

August is the end of our summer!) We're in the middle of another lovely spell of weather, and praying it will hold for Lucy's wedding on 8 July. Sarah, being a marriage commissioner, will conduct the marriage service in Atlin on board the *Tarahne*, an ancient lake boat hauled up on ways. She does weddings very nicely in her own unique style, and with a plummy voice into the bargain. She has performed them in some fairly exotic places – in the middle of the suspension footbridge that spans Miles Canyon; by helicopter to the top of Golden Horn mountain; at the Marsh Lake marina. I put my foot down when a couple asked her to marry them canoeing down the Wheaton River because she's a gunwale-grabber when it comes to white-water. Given the chance she'd probably have performed one free-fall above the Carcross Desert.

Wedding arrangements have kept the women of the family engrossed for weeks and, not wanting to spoil their fun, I have kept clear of it – sexist pig that I am. I have one big decision to make: do I take them away from the dock after the wedding ceremony in our little green tugboat, *Loon Dancer*, or do I sail them away in my sailboat, *Arctic Tern*? It's a bit like offering your teenager, who's threatening to leave home – the red suitcase or the blue suitcase.

Before we left the UK I gave away the old morning dress tails suit I was married in to kids of Bristol friends for dressing up games (same syndrome as burning the kilt). When Lucy and Alain visited the friends recently they dug the suit out of a cupboard – the jacket fitted Alain perfectly, though the trousers needed shortening. Lucy is borrowing a friend's Laura Ashley white wedding gown, notwithstanding they've been living together for seven years. Maybe they've got it better figured out than we had. As far as Sarah and I can remember, the most pressing need for us to get married was so that we could cohabit legally – not the soundest reasoning for a lifetime commitment. However it seemed to work.

Recently we've spent all our weekends in Atlin. Sarah loves it there. One day, Robert, you must come and visit our little corner of paradise. First, you'll have to read about it in the fall when *Atlin's Gold* comes out. I've just talked with Caitlin Press and everything seems to be on schedule. They are such pleasant and professional people to deal with. I've almost forgotten that I wrote the damned book, and can hardly remember what's in it. Funny, that's the same experience I've had with the other books I have written.

I've been rather impatient with her lately, and feel bad when I do. She's got used to calling for me from her bed. Unwittingly she continues to command the same attention, and I cannot always give it immediately. I find it hard to know how much to pander to her whims, selfless person that she is, how much to work at retaining my own sanity in order to be able to care for her when things get really bad.

Thank you so much for reading the manuscript of 'my story.' I'm ashamed to call it autobiography; perhaps memoir is more apt. Everyone writes those. I've been reading chapters to Sarah, and it's amazing how many repeat words, frank mistakes, and errors of rhythm one picks up when reading aloud. I'll probably close this volume on our leaving for Nepal just after we were married. Then I'll start on a second episode. I don't expect to find a publisher here in Canada because it would be of interest mostly in Britain where the action lies. Perhaps some good editor might be able to knock it into manageable form one day. Publication is not the sole object of the exercise; it's important for me to keep that in mind, otherwise I'll start writing for an audience rather than letting it flow unimpeded. Whatever happens, the original version will be for the children to read in order to get some picture of their dad. Is this important, I wonder, or just personal vanity?

I'm so enjoying working two and a half days a week, and don't miss carrying other people's problems home with me at night. My colleagues have deeply furrowed brows and shoulders stooped under the burdens of the world. On my writing days I try to be at my desk at 8 a.m. and work through till midday. Then I feel I've done a good day's work, and I may do a little correcting in the afternoon. I do much better with structure, having led a structured life for so long.

Judith and I have been busy flagging my new ski trail on the top of the hill round which our main 10 km trail lies. For several years I have explored the forest up there. It is full of big old-growth pine, spruce, aspen and silver birch – never logged because it's so inaccessible. Getting away into the woods in utter peace for a few hours is very therapeutic for me, and is a great chance to talk with Judith. We are trying to cut only willow brush and as few trees as possible. I'd love to name it after Sarah when it's finished. Every day when I get home I tell her what we have done anew.

Letter #16

Whitehorse, 16 July '95

My dear Robert,

Our news is all WEDDING! Lucy was married by Sarah, as marriage commissioner, on 8 July. It was a magical day with Atlin looking its perfect best, and a slight breeze to keep the bugs away. I still haven't found a single more magnificent place in the world. Forest fires had raged for the previous week, so haze had obscured the mountains across the lake. However, on Saturday the air was clear, and the sky remained cloudless until nightfall.

The preparations seem to have been going on for weeks. It was mostly a do-it-yourself wedding, which made it more intimate. Alain and Lucy had made all their own wine; Judith baked and iced the cake; local friends provided the flowers; a hairdresser friend did the girls' hair; Hector lent the tents; a local Atlin lady catered for the party. Everyone in town was involved in some way or another.

On the evening before the wedding we had a potluck supper on the deck of the cabin for Alain's Quebecois family, and all the out-oftowners. The Quebec flag flew from the flagpole beside the cabin. The Rompkeys, friends from our Labrador days, came from Ottawa where Bill had been an MP for over 20 years; he was formerly the North West River school principal and choirmaster - and once turned me down for the church choir! Sarah's nephew, Tom Martin, came from Hong Kong where he is an officer in the Gurkhas. Caroline Kennard flew up from Victoria. Seven of Lucy's old team-mates on the national cross-country ski team came up from Alberta and BC, along with one of Alain's companions from Quebec. Atlin was throbbing with jocks, so on the morning of the wedding I took them for a hike up Monarch Mountain to let them burn off some energy.

Sarah helped Lucy get dressed in Noland House, a posh B&B at the other end of town, where they were going to spend their nuptial night. It's only four blocks away from the cabin, and the town is so small you can almost shout across it. Lucy looked stunning in her Laura Ashley dress that had been re-whitened and pressed by a friend who is a professional fabric restorer. Its very low-cut back showed her bulging shoulder muscles rippling every time she moved her arms. Her hair was done up on the back of her head, and she wore a coronet of wild flowers. We felt mighty proud of her.

At 3:45 p.m. I collected Lucy from Noland House with her escort of Judith, carrying Rosie, grandson Tim's miniature dachshund. Tim clutched a cushion, with the rings firmly secured, and with the other hand held a niece and nephew of Alain. I wore my own wedding going-away suit of 34 years, with turn-ups and bell-bottoms that I could roll up to my knees – very useful on the boat. I laid out a scarlet Hudson's Bay blanket on the dock as a red carpet.

Lucy sat on a sheepskin on the foredeck of *Loon Dancer* looking like a princess; Judith was in the back with the kids, all wearing life jackets. As skipper, I wore my new yellow survival suit and Rod Tuck's old Royal Marines hat. We cruised past the *Tarahne*, the boat built in 1930 to ply the lake, and now laid up ashore on way blocks. She is being restored, and was newly white-painted last year. All the guests gathered on the decks and waved at Lucy. We tied up in front of Kirkwood's Cottages at our usual moorage where Lucy had to negotiate the ladder in high heels and hooped wedding dress – no sweat for an athlete.

Then we paraded back to the *Tarahne*, where Adam, who had come over from Montreal, welcomed all the guests on the foredeck. Sarah had got her Yukon marriage commissioner's license extended for the day as a special favour. Because she couldn't stand for long she perched herself on a high stool and appeared magisterial in a dark blue suit. Alain looked a million dollars wearing my tails suit, and was surprisingly nervous despite having competed in several Olympic Games and World Championships.

Sarah read her marriage ceremony sounding, as usual, like Queen Elizabeth giving her Christmas address to the Empire. She skipped a page in the middle, missing a crucial part of the vows, which was bossily corrected by the bride, who stepped forward with a loud, "Oh! Mother!" Hoots of mirth from the assembled company. Alain's sister translated Sarah's text into French as Sarah read along out loud. About 140 people were on the boat.

After the exchange of vows and rings, and signing of the register, Archie Knill took photos on the afterdeck under the old BC flag, which has the Union Jack prominently in one corner. Then Lucy and Alain walked through Atlin, with townspeople clapping and cheering, to the reception in the recreation park, where their team-mates had made an arch of skis for them to walk under.

It was a perfect sunny evening so everyone ate outside at tables decorated with wild flowers. Across the fence was a huge children's playground, built with money willed by an old bachelor prospector, so all the kids could entertain themselves safely while their parents watched. David Howe gave a very funny speech to the bride. I gave a short account in French of how, when I went to watch her in Thunder Bay, she uttered the classic statement about Alain: "Soon he's going to be my husband, then I can boss him around." I presented him with a montage of photos Judith had taken of Lucy, aged about ten, pulling dreadful faces – a secret weapon for him to use when she gets too uppity. Luckily he's a very peaceable, accommodating fellow.

During the reception Sarah sat in a large garden chair and held court for all her friends. It was a lovely occasion and I felt mighty proud of the family. Sarah has been running on adrenaline for a month, so she's quite whacked now. However, it was worth it for her being so utterly absorbed in the planning and execution of it all. She has had some new pains in her other hip, and her tumour-marker cell count has risen, so she's going down to Vancouver on Tuesday for some more X-rays, and possibly a jag of radiation.

Robert, I worry now because I'm so numb and I barely raise a tear over everything that is happening to Sarah. I guess in a way I'm fortifying myself unconsciously for tough days ahead, but I don't like feeling so utterly empty of emotion. Worse, Sarah and I have been getting up each other's noses of late with all the wedding activity, and I'm not very good at dealing with that. Partly it's because we are together so much, and on top of each other without enough space of our own. I need to be around her constantly for all the routine things of keeping the home together and ticking over. Morphine in continuous doses seems to make her more irritable than she ever was before. I'm sure she's well-and-truly hooked on it now. Perhaps I'm just being less tolerant. Not being able to get around as spryly as she used to, she tends to call from her bed, and I can't always jump to, then and there. The wedding has put a lot of strain on everybody (good strain at that), and now that things have quietened down, perhaps we'll get back on a more even keel.

I am sure you know how hard it is living with someone who is ill and is inexorably dying. I almost feel guilty for being so healthy. Then I tell myself that I cannot live her illness for her. In fact, I mustn't try because I have to be there to be strong when things really start to fall apart. I also know I have to allow myself time on my own to gain strength for the final lap.

We are planning to go to the UK in late September, via Montreal, for Adam's wedding. He announced a month or so ago that he was getting married in the fall. Oh, yeah, pull the other one! He's had a succession of such weird girl friends I was only going to believe it when it happened. The 'python lady,' who came a couple of years ago dressed in slinky black and high heels, and wound herself round him from morning till night (wanting it *all* the time, he assured me – how can anyone be so lucky?). She stuffed food into her face, licked her fingers continually, and was utterly useless on the sailboat – the #1 criterion for acceptance into the family.

Then there was the 'box lady' who collected cardboard boxes full of old magazines and newspapers, which she stacked in his apartment until there was no floor space left. She moved out with two truckloads of boxes. On the boat she wore a stupid hat sprouting Achilles's wings, and sat in the cockpit with her legs crossed so I tripped over them whenever I had to manoeuvre. She, too, was written off.

Louise, his fiancée, is quite normal – and a very good crew on *Arctic Tern*, who passed with flying colours. She's a lawyer in a high-tech computer firm where they both work. They met at a business lunch, had dinner a week later, and bought the ring the next day! She came for a week after Lucy's wedding, very sensibly, because she would have been overwhelmed by scores of strange family and friends. We had a very good trip down the lake in sunshine and a howling wind.

Sarah and I are going to the wedding, to be conducted by the Finnish Lutheran chaplain of Concordia University. Then we fly over to the UK two days later on 18 September. We'll visit her mother and many friends in the south of England. Then, depending on how she's doing, we'll go into Wales, or even Ireland, for a few days. It's still uncertain if the Bhutan trip will go, as there were not enough sign-ups when the company last wrote. If it doesn't I'll possibly get a rail pass and visit our friend Vladimir in Prague; then up to Lithuania to stay with my old schoolfriend, Rod Tuck. Who knows? I might just keep going to Moscow and then catch the Trans Siberian to Vladivostok.

I'm sure we'll get down to Hornby sometime on the fall. The Denman Lighthouse painting reminds us of your dear house and of our happy visits to you.

Letter #17

Whitehorse, 18 Aug. '95

My dear Robert,

Many thanks for your letter of 23 July. Things have settled down no end since the wedding. Sarah is back to her old considerate self, and the tension engendered by all the arrangements has subsided. She is using Fentanyl skin patches instead of morphine to control her pain, and being off the morphine seems to suit her much better. She only uses morphine for a top-up now and again if she's going out or doing something special. She's had occasions of being quite confused and forgetting things, which is quite unlike her – and causes me concern. Her other hip has been troublesome so she's going down to Vancouver on Sunday for another jag of radiation; then home on Monday evening.

We'll fly to Montreal on 14 September for Adam's wedding. The Bhutan trip is off, but we are going to the UK anyway. I plan to be there a full month so there will be no pressure of time if Sarah has to lie up and rest for a few days. She can then have long, uninterrupted gossips with her mother and her sister. I don't know how much she'll be able to do, but we'll just play it by ear. She's much more crippled than when we were with you.

She has persuaded me that she can manage to return home from England by herself, I feel alright about this as the girls can look after her when she gets back here. Frankly, I need a break from the humdrum, day-by-day, fetch and carry. Doesn't that sound selfish piggery? I don't think the kids know what it's like to be on call 24 hours a day. They're excellent at blowing in and out, and doing anything we ask, so I don't want to sound ungrateful. I'll also arrange for friends to call frequently; and her best friend, Kathy, is coming over from Juneau for a few days.

Fall has come two weeks early here, the trees are beginning to change colour, and there's a nip of autumn in the air.

Letter #18

Whitehorse, 7 Sept. '95

My dear Robert,

Herewith the promised letter to follow up the note I sent you. Our living room is almost like being in your dining area. On one wall we have Denman Lighthouse with the waves crashing on the rocks and the mountains behind; on another wall Fen's new picture as if we were about to walk into the cedar forest behind your house – reminiscent of an Emily Carr painting, but less sombre.

To recap the two awful weeks that have passed is like a bad dream. Sarah went down to Vancouver on Sunday evening, ostensibly for a single radiation treatment to her hip on the Monday and return home the same day. However, her doctors decided that four treatments might be more effective, so she stayed over in a hotel near the Cancer Hospital. She slipped in the bath and couldn't get out because she fractured her shoulder in the fall. She lay there for quite some time, as she said, "…like a beached whale." Luckily she had a lunch date with her friend, Polly, who, finding she was late, called the hotel and insisted they go up to investigate. Sarah was admitted directly to the hospital; they did further X-rays and found a bunch of new lesions in her spine, hip, and chest.

Then she started doing strange things, and being very forgetful and confused – both, with hindsight, symptoms I had occasionally noticed during the previous couple of months, but which I had put down to the effects of morphine. What really alerted the doctors to something seriously wrong was when she was asking her breakfast nurse where her boiled egg was, all the time holding it in her left hand. She was also having trouble with print on the page fading to the left side. She had a CT scan of her brain and they found one lesion in her cerebellum (concerned with balance), another in her occipital cortex (concerned with vision), and a lot of brain swelling. I'm telling you this story so coldly, yet it was a cataclysmic blow to find what I had suspected for a while – that she has metastases, or spread, in her brain. It was like a death sentence, after several reprieves.

I booted it down to Vancouver, and was with her when Dr Susan O'Reilly told her the bad news, matter-of-factly, compassionately, sitting on her bed and holding her hand. "What a nuisance!" was all she said. She told me later that she shed buckets of tears in the night, with her Greek room-mate, Maria, who was very comforting to her. Sarah knew the score, but she never let me see how upset she was.

Strangely we all seem to have accepted the diagnosis for what it is, and are just getting on with things as normal. The girls were distraught to begin with, but they seem to have come to terms with the situation. The reality is that it will be a miracle if Sarah is still here next spring to go on our planned visit to her birthplace in Cyprus. I know she's dying, yet she's so very much alive, still far more concerned with other people's worries than her own, still scheming far into the future.

I've given a lot of thought to what you and I talked about on the cliff path in Helliwell Park on Hornby. When the time is right for her I feel pretty certain she will make me promise to ensure she doesn't suffer, and to bring her travail to a close. She knows I have the wherewithal in my black medical bag, and the knowledge – what a privilege! I don't think I would have any difficulty in carrying out her wish, but faced with the reality of snuffing out the life of the person I most love in the world may be a tall order. That is a far more solemn contract than any opinion the law may impose, and frankly it would only fleetingly cross my mind that the law and I might not be on the same track. Whether I will be so bold in the event is uncertain. She must have the right to control what is happening to her body, and if the pain is unbearable and she wants an exit I feel obliged to honour her wish. Who am I to deny her the control she has striven for all these painful months? But it is not easy to kill someone, and I have to be resolute and sure of success.

Since we returned home Sarah is comfortably installed in her bed on the floor, and is her usual jaunty, cheerful self. We are busy planning our trip to Britain, and talking of a visit to Victoria in December, and a visit to Cyprus next spring to see her birthplace. This all seems so important that we should look forward to every day as a new adventure. We can deal with the problems as they arise, but for the moment we are living as vividly as we can with every wonderful moment left to us together.

Two weeks ago my eyes were constantly brimful of tears, my voice would crack at most inauspicious moments, and I would cry uncontrollably whenever someone was nice to me. Now I seem to be surrounded again by my own impervious shell, like a carapace that lets me function despite the spectre hanging over us. I try to imagine what goes on in Sarah's mind, because she has such a stoic front that I could easily be deceived into thinking she hasn't a worry in the world. However, I can't comprehend it. Her pain seems to be under control, she is alert, and her balance is better. We are off to Montreal for Adam's wedding, then on to England on Sunday. Sarah wants to take the night sleeper (First Class) to Scotland, so that is a jaunt to look forward to.

LETTER #19

LONDON, 4 OCT. '95

My dear Robert,

We've had a wonderful holiday and Sarah stood up to it well considering we toured much of the British Isles. You'll have to excuse a rather long-winded account of our travels, which might be good to read in bed because it may put you to sleep.

First, we flew to Montreal for Adam's wedding that was totally different from Lucy's. We stayed in Adam's apartment, a huge open studio room on the seventh floor of an old garment factory at the corner of St Laurent and Duluth. He can walk a couple of blocks to reach the foot of Mount Royal. We propped Sarah up in a big bed they had made up in the middle of the room so she could rest up before the wedding next day. She looked out over the whole east of the city, with lots of greenery in the parks that I have not seen before because I have always visited in winter. She held court in her accustomed fashion, surrounded by family and friends.

Louise gave our girls, as a present, sessions with a coiffeuse, so they spent half the day downtown in a beauty salon. Sarah was unable to take up the gift as her hair is beginning to fall out after her chemo and radiation. She and I took a cab to the posh hotel where Adam and Louise were going to stay after the ceremony. Louise looked stunning in a magenta shot-silk dress and shawl: Adam was unusually svelte. When the girls rolled through the swing doors of the hotel foyer after their treatment I nearly keeled over because one looked like a Barbie doll, the other a high-class hooker. They don't often get the chance to get really tarted up, and they had so much fun in doing it.

Adam and Louise had rented a wheelchair for Sarah, and a white stretch limousine to take us to the Loyola Campus of Concordia University where Adam is studying. We all piled in, and Sarah was dreadfully sick, partly from the undulations of the limo, partly the after-effects of radiation. As usual, she shrugged it off as if it was just a minor inconvenience. We carried her up the steps of the university ecumenical chapel for the service conducted by a pastor with barely a mention of God. Adam read from John Donne, and Louise recited some French poetry. The best man, Terry, had recently narrowly escaped being shot by madman Fabrikant in the engineering department of Concordia, on a day when Adam, who was heading to visit Terry, on a whim decided to go home instead.

After the wedding a party of close friends and family went to a restaurant in Old Montreal (in the limo driving more sedately this time) for a feast. Sarah had thoroughly enjoyed the day but was quite tired so went home early by cab with Lucy. We doggie-bagged the dessert of strawberry chocolate gateau for her. She spent most of the next day resting in preparation for our long flight to Europe, while I ambled round the streets of Montreal with Adam and had a long talk about his mum. He was fully aware of the seriousness of her condition and was very supportive. I had a cry on his shoulder; not a role I'm accustomed to with him, but very comforting.

Next morning we saw Adam and Louise off to Cuba on their honeymoon. Then we prepared to catch our plane from Dorval airport. It's no cakewalk handling someone solo in a wheelchair in a city. We called a cab, and I had the luggage downstairs waiting. Then I took Sarah down to the cab, but I had to return the rented wheelchair to Adam's apartment. I didn't want to lose the elevator at the seventh floor so I folded my leather jacket hoping it would block the automatic doors from closing while I dashed into the apartment to leave the chair. When I returned the door had squeezed my coat tight so I had difficulty extracting it, and it jiggered up the works so the door wouldn't open at all. Leaving the disabled elevator, I ran down seven floors hoping not to meet in the hallway angry tenants waiting for the lift that would never come.

At the airport the cab driver had put us down well away from the main doors. I left Sarah sitting on our baggage while I dashed across two roads to the main building to find a wheelchair. I piled the luggage onto a trolley, and Sarah into the chair. Then, driving one with each hand in tandem, negotiated her across the traffic and into the terminal. Without wanting to bore you with mundane travel stories, Robert, this was only the beginning of an epic.

We arrived late in Toronto because of work on the runways, so had a very short time before our London flight should leave. I had to pick up our tickets from a desk in the airport terminal, so left Sarah with an airline staffer to mind her while I sprinted to the Canadian Airlines desk. Being a Sunday evening, all offices were shut and there were no tickets to collect at the check-in counter, so we missed the flight. I had Sarah on the other side of the airport and eventually the minder brought her to where I was waiting. We were bundled onto a flight to Paris with only a coupon for tickets, but we were upgraded to business class, which made the flight more comfortable. In Paris a young Algerian porter blasted his way through all the desk clerks, who shrugged negatively at our coupon. We reached London only a few hours after our original intended time of arrival. Our luggage didn't arrive, but caught up with us next day via the *Pony Express*. Sarah was exhausted but still able to enjoy the adventure, reminiscent of many travels we have done in recent years – but not in a wheelchair!

We picked up our rental car at Heathrow and drove straight to Bungay, the Suffolk home of Sarah's mother, Irene, who is a hale 86. She had made up a bed for Sarah in the glass-roofed conservatory, looking out on the garden. Rain made a pattering noise on the glass, and Sarah could watch it splattering overhead. It was an ideal place for her to get over jet lag and to spend unhurried time with her mother. As much as possible I left them alone to chat, and drove myself through Norfolk lanes to Norwich, and drank Guinness at the local pub. The publican had once been in the Mounties at Medicine Hat.

While resting, Sarah was fair. She didn't eat much because of the nausea from her treatments, and she was occasionally quite confused, which was worrying – more for her mother than for me, as I was used to these lapses. We planned to return to Irene at the end of our holiday, so we set off for London and drove south under wide Suffolk skies on a perfect sunny day when ploughmen were followed by clouds of seagulls.

We visited Bury St Edmunds, near where we lived just after we were married, and where I did spells in obstetrics and anaesthetics. I wheeled Sarah round the lovely old market town we knew so well, and visited Great St Mary's Church where once I climbed up repair-scaffolding under the roof to photograph the carved angels and animals for my boss, a keen photographer, who was afraid of heights.

Then we drove five miles south of Bury to see The Bakery,

Shoemeadow Bottom, Chevington, a thatched cottage that was the first home we ever bought – for £2,000. Last time we were there some years ago it looked very run down, but was now for sale – asking price £275,000! It had been lovingly restored by a young couple who ran The Tiger Trust out of an office in the old garage where I used to keep my Austin Seven coupé. I would drive it to work in Bury with a cork stuffed into the radiator. The willow trees we had planted beside the pond were huge, and the tiny River Lark ran through the seven-acre field that bordered the vast Ickworth estate from where pheasants used to sneak onto our lawn to avoid the shooting parties. We spent a few very happy years there on and off, interrupted in 1961 by driving overland to Nepal in our Land Rover.

We drove over to nearby Denston Church where we were married in one of the most perfect small mediaeval churches I know (my hobby used to be exploring ancient churches and buildings). It had been carefully restored and cleaned with newly whitewashed walls and brightly embroidered kneelers. We stood at the altar where we took our vows, sunshine piercing the stained glass. She took my hand, and said, "It's been a wonderful thirty-four years, darling" – the only time she ever spoke in the past tense. It choked me up. I gave her a big hug, and she said, "I don't want to cry now." It was an intense shared moment, and I knew she was not ready to talk about it any more then.

I wheeled her across the graveyard to look for the headstone with two of our babies' names on it – Benjamin, who was buried in North West River, Labrador; and Ruth here in Denston. It was encrusted with lichen that I tried to brush off. "Poor little toots," she said, "but we'd never have had Judith if they'd lived." Ever positive, as was her way.

We drove to nearby Stansfield where Sarah's parents house, *Bridgman's*, stood, scene of our first courting days ('hedging and ditching' we called it), and where we had the reception after our wedding. The countryside was as beautiful as ever, rolling Suffolk hillocks under wide cloud-laden skies. Our final call was to the Bell Inn, Clare, a small town nearby where we had our wedding dance and spent the first night of our honeymoon. In lowering light we headed for London, and navigated by the sun and Sarah's excellent map reading to the Barbor house in Islington – bang on!

Tricia Barbor tucked Sarah up on the couch in the kitchen, and all the family gathered round for supper. She loves being surrounded by people, talking and laughing. Sadly, Peter Barbor was away working in Saudi Arabia, but he phoned in the evening. Sarah was very tired after our long trip down Memory Lane, but it was such a cheerful day for the most part, always remembering the funny and ridiculous rather than dwelling on her present sad state.

On a beautiful day we wended our way to Bristol to stay with the Keelings, some of Sarah's closest friends. She sat in bed catching up with Joan on the gossip about all our other friends – the spicier the better. We drove round Canynge Square, where we lived for eight years before we moved to Canada – the longest stay in any one place in our lives! Then to Clifton village where Sarah had a stall in the antiques market. John James, a doctor friend and neighbour, examined Sarah and, after consulting an oncologist colleague, put her back on the full dose of dexamethasone steroid as he reckoned it was so important for her to be alert in order to enjoy this very special holiday.

I saw three of my ex-bosses. Denis Bodenham gave me news of the successes of all the Frenchay Hospital plastic surgery residents scattered around the globe.

"I must be the only failure among them," I observed. "Not at all," he said, "you and Sarah have had such an interesting and exciting life together." On reflection, I had to agree.

We crossed the Severn Bridge into South Wales on a magical stormy day, with clouds racing overhead and black thunderstorms hovering between patches of sunlight. We had lunch at a pub in Brecon, where I was offered a job in 1975 – but came to Canada instead. We wondered how the kids would have turned out if we had stayed. They certainly wouldn't have had all the exciting opportunities they've enjoyed in the Yukon. We visited Philip Morgan, the farmer whose cottages we used to rent – Bleinau Uchaf, and then Blencar. I parked the car beside a small ford we used to drive across below the house, and left Sarah to sleep in the sun while I walked alongside the stream that descends from Carmarthen Fan. The kids would jump into a swirling pool made in a rock and overhung by mountain ash trees heavy with red berries. They were peaceful retreats from our busy surgical life in Bristol. We returned via Hay-on-Wye, Llantony Abbey, the Wye Valley, and Tintern Abbey. We had so many happy reminiscences, and Sarah stood up to the twelve-hour day amazingly well.

After lots of rest and laughs with Joan Keeling in Bristol we drove up to London to stay with Sarah's sister, Jean. I went off to Lithuania to visit my oldest schoolmate, Rod Tuck, who was teaching English to technical college students – the prettier the better. The country, so recently released from Russian oppression, was exulting in its freedom, yet not sure what to do with it. Mafia crime is rampant, creaming the economy and leaving the citizens pitifully poor. Vilnius and Kaunas are beautiful old cities with huge pedestrian precincts, avenues of trees, and green parks. Ballet and opera alternate, and there's a philharmonic concert hall just down the road – a seat in the stalls costs $3.

I bought for Sarah some amber jewellery collected on the Baltic coast; one piece has a 10,000 years old fly embedded in it. The heating isn't turned on in Rod's primitive apartment block until the end of October, so I froze and was glad I had taken my longjohns.

I'm now back in London, so I'll draw this letter to a close. But,

Robert, let me tell you we're having the holiday of our lives, and in its own way as enjoyable as any of those we've had before. I hope things are well on Hornby, and that your eyes are alright.

LETTER #20

WHITEHORSE, 18 OCT. '95

My dear Robert,

Sarah and I are back from our holiday – and what a tour it was! I last wrote from London on my return from Lithuania, so I will bring you up to date with the latter part of our promenade.

During the time I was away Sarah had a grand time quilting with her sister, Jean. In the week together they had unhurried time to forge a special bond without their usual sisterly rivalries. Then we went off on our overnight train journey to Scotland. At home in Whitehorse Sarah had read an account of the trip in the *Manchester Guardian Weekly*. She decided that was what she wanted to do, so I bought two four-day BritRail passes – First Class.

On our way to Euston station we dropped in on my first medicine boss at St George's Hospital, Tooting – Sir John Batten – to whom I sold my turquoise Austin-Healey 3000, that immediately thereafter broke down. JB (as he was known) was the Queen's Physician for a decade, and he told us of the time his beeper went off as he was just about to address a meeting of the Royal College of Physicians.

Princess: "Doctor, my maid has piles, what shall I do?"

JB: "I'm sure it can wait till morning, ma'am."

JB wheeled Sarah through Kew Gardens, nearby his house, always dashing at top speed as he used to do on ward rounds at Tooting. What a privilege to have worked for such a man – the best boss I ever had.

Euston. First Class sleeper to Inverness. Clickety-click (not clackety-clack), so quiet and smooth we could barely tell when the train was moving as it pulled out of a station. I tucked Sarah into her bunk with the adjoining door between our compartments open, and went down to the buffet bar to fetch her a gin-and-tonic. In the corridor I bumped into Chris Brasher, a climbing friend who I had not seen for 25 years.

CB: "This deserves champagne. Go and grab a chair over there while I call my racehorse trainer in Newmarket. By the way, put a fiver each way on *Maid of the Hills*: Redcar, 3:45 Thursday."

Brasher puts through a couple more calls on his mobile phone – one to our mutual friend Eric Langmuir in Aviemore where we are bound – but the call gets cut off when we entered a tunnel.

Sarah and I wake in Carlisle. Next, at Killiekrankie, we hear a knock at the door and a tall Indian steward (who surely must have once worked the *Rajdhani Express*) hands in a cup of tea and a croissant. "Aviemore in half an hour," he says.

By 8 a.m. Sarah was sitting in front of Eric's picture window, looking out over Avielochan to the Cairngorms, dark in stormy high winds, and clouds racing across the tops. We both felt thoroughly refreshed after our night on the train. Sarah spent time resting in Eric's beautiful modern house and chatting with his family. Three of Eric's kids were on the British alpine ski team, one racing at the Albertville

Olympics when Lucy was also competing there.

Eric and I did a good day hike above Aviemore. His wife, Maureen, died of breast cancer ten years ago, when their kids were still quite young. Previously we have had some long talks about his travails; this time it was my turn to pour out my heart to his understanding ears. I am still deeply concerned as to how I will manage if Sarah asks to make sure she doesn't suffer. I find I have to be discriminating with whom I talk because few people can really understand what you are going through unless they have experienced it themselves. Eric could.

On our second day Sarah and I took the twin-carriage day train to Skye – First Class, of course. We travelled with the wheelchair for changing trains in Inverness. Then on a sunny, windy day with ochre bracken and most of the heather over, our little train sauntered across the Highlands stopping at every wayside halt and station. At the Kyle of Lochalsh Hotel we had lunch of heavy mulligatawny soup. While looking for the new bridge to the Isle of Skye, I pushed Sarah up and down every hill in town laughing like schoolkids looking for kicks.

We bought Sarah a Black Watch tam o'shanter, as her hair is falling out fast after the chemo and radiation but she never complains about it. She cut off the bobble, and looks smashing in the beret. Then we returned on the 5 p.m. train, which ground to a halt, with brake failure, 300 yards from Aviemore. We were stuck for an hour and a half, and could see the lights of Eric's house. We could have crossed the fields if it hadn't been for the wheelchair. What a wonderfully happy adventure that day was!

Next day Eric and I joined Brasher and friends to hike over Fannich Mhor near Ullapool in a howling gale that churned the lakes into whitecaps, throwing spume 100 feet high, and blowing the waterfalls vertically. How I love the Highlands – they are so like parts of the Yukon. Sarah rested up and enjoyed the chance to be alone.

Sadly, we left Eric, his partner, Marion, and the young Langmuirs and took the train to Edinburgh by day so we could enjoy the scenery. We embarked on an open-topped, double-decker bus tour round the city, the guide telling us of every grizzly murder in its history – Burke & Hare, Jekyll & Hyde – and recitations of Burns's '*Wee sleekit, cowrin', timorous beastie*' and Abe Lincoln's *Gettysburg Address* (for the Yanks). We passed Surgeons' Hall, scene of my only surgical triumph – the Fellowship of the Royal College of Surgeons, Edin. Then at great speed in Sarah's jalopy we went down Princes' Street, dodging rush hour pedestrians, to buy for me some Black Watch tartan boxer shorts at Marks & Spencer.

We had dinner at the old North British Hotel – now the Balmoral (Forte) – built over Waverley station. Last time I was there, was on return from a climbing trip to Skye, smelly and wearing my grandfather's kilt:

PS (in plummy English) to doorman: "Can I rent a bath here, please?"

Kilted Doorman: "Ye can that, laddie, but ye're no a trrrue Scotsman!"

Then the night sleeper – First Class, don't forget – to Euston. We spent a few more days in Bungay with Sarah's mother, Irene. They had a gossipy time together reminiscing about Cyprus (where Sarah was born, and her father, Mac, was in the Colonial Service) and Nigeria where he was posted. To keep out of the way I went to the Hearts of Oak pub round the corner for a pint of draught Guinness. Sarah needed a good rest after all our gallivanting of the past week.

When Sarah said goodbye to her mother it was just a routine farewell like all the others she has made to friends. She knows, her mother knows, and I know, that it's probably her last farewell. We just drive off down the road with a wave, and on to the next stop on our itinerary. Never a tear or a moan – I can barely hold my own back.

We drove to Cambridge where I pushed Sarah in her wheelchair round the Backs in low-slung, soft autumnal sun with mists rising off the River Cam. First, through Trinity, past the Wren Library where as undergraduates on Sunday mornings we used to practice traversing the base of the pillar a foot above ground; then past King's Chapel to the meadows: across Clare Bridge, to feel the stone ball with the slice cut out of it. Clare was utterly lovely. How lucky I was to have been an undergraduate there. Finally, through Trinity Hall, where one of Sarah's many swains had rooms.

Sarah was in Cambridge, aged seventeen, doing a secretarial course. She stayed with Mrs Bevan, who ran a paying guest house for classy foreign girls with a few ordinary English girls thrown in for good measure. Dr Bevan was rowing coach of the Blue Boat, so the girls were never lost for escorts. Irene once said to Sarah before her exams, "Don't you think you'd better do some work, darling?" The reply: "Oh, but I don't have time for work, Mummy."

Then we drove down to London, past the pubs and Wren churches where we used to go courting on Sundays when the City was deserted. I parked Sarah with her sister, Jean, near Hampton Court, while I went up to London.

In Tite St, Phyllis Wint, Eric Shipton's lady of twenty years, persuaded me to have another crack at writing Eric's biography. Her basement flat is just down the street from Wilfred Thesiger's lofty penthouse. Once Eric and Wilfred met in the street: WT wearing a dark suit, rolled umbrella, and bowler hat; ES in a polo neck pullover, sports coat and cords.

WT to ES: "You can't walk round London like that!"

I had lunch with Wilfred at his flat from which he has a view of the River Thames, a corner of the Albert Bridge, and the tops of the trees in the Chelsea Physic Garden. Wilfred helped me plan our Tibesti trip across the Sahara in 1957, being the only person who had previously travelled through the area. He is 85 and has a magnificent rugged face with a scar down his right cheek (duelling or a Bedouin's bullet?), the apocryphal Thesiger nose accentuated by being broken when boxing for Oxford against Cambridge. We talked and talked.

Sarah and I last saw Wilfred in Kenya in 1989. He had to leave Maralal because his eyes were failing and his extended family had broken up. Sadly the journey through Afghanistan we planned to do together many years ago never came off. To have travelled with such a Titan would have been an amazing experience – but probably I couldn't have kept up.

I also met Margaret Body, my editor at Hodder & Stoughton – now Hodder Headline, that produces quick-sell, soft porn books that Sarah always buys for long plane flights. Maggie also encouraged me to pursue the Shipton biography.

So our magical action-packed month came to an end and Sarah and I flew across half the world back to our little tin house in the Yukon. We've had such a wonderful holiday and each day we recall some incident or other that keeps the memory alive.

LETTER #21

WHITEHORSE, 26 OCT. '95

My dear Robert,

Sarah has taken a sudden turn for the worse. She started becoming confused a couple of days ago, then vomited sporadically. She's been sleeping during most of the day, waking confused and unable to remember the names of things or to complete a sentence. In the night her breathing was irregular, like Cheyne-Stokes periodic pattern of stops and starts. These are all bad signs of what is going on inside her head. Either they mean the swelling, that was reduced by the dexamethasone, has returned, or that the tumour has extended along with more swelling. Whatever the cause, the outlook is grim. I called Dr Susan O'Reilly who wants her to increase the dexamethasone in the hope that it will diminish the swelling again, and make her more lucid. The confusion bothers her a lot because she knows what she wants to say but can't get it together. Susan thinks it may also be caused by a rise in her blood calcium.

I've never watched someone close to me dying, Robert, and it's devastating. Here I am trying to appear to have it all together, and then I go into my study and tears pour down my cheeks onto the paper. I can't believe that our partnership, which has been through so much together, is now about to be rent asunder. I hug her in bed and feel her warm and soft, and I know that in a short while she will be no more. What a joy that I can be in bed with her for ten hours at a time, and able to stroke and hug her, rather than have her in a cold, clinical hospital bed. I'll never let that happen, come what may.

I'm trying to be practical and think what to do when Sarah dies. Her will says she wishes to be cremated, but faced with the reality of having to ship her off to Prince George in a box to some uncaring incinerator – Whitehorse can't do it yet – I can't countenance anything so impersonal. The kids and I agree we will bury her and thereby make our own shrine. I had thought we would take her down Atlin Lake to Steele Island, but it is important for us all to be able to visit her grave. So I'm going to arrange for a spot in the Atlin Cemetery. Atlin has been so much the focus of our family life here in the North that I think it is where she would like to lie – and me beside her when my time comes – so I've bought a double plot.

God, it's wrenching planning your own wife's farewell when she's lying in the next room, still alive. I don't want any palaver. Just a plain wooden box, and we will take her down in the back of my little car, not in some bloody hearse of a faceless funeral parlour. I don't want anyone else to lay a hand on her. And I'll keep her here in her own bed till the very last moment if I can possibly manage it.

28 Oct. '95

The dexamethasone should have kicked in by now if it was going to – but it hasn't. So I fear Sarah's confusion is due to an extension of the tumours we know are inside her head. She's totally muddled about time, people, events, but it doesn't appear to cause her as much anxiety as when she was more alert. Her pain seems to be under control. She just passes the time in a peaceful haze, occasionally emerging from it. Audrey McLaughlin just called by and Sarah perked up for about ten minutes, appearing her normal gossipy self. But she soon relapsed when Audrey left.

In the morning I went out to my neophyte ski trail along with a man driving a huge front-end loader lent by a construction firm to pull a lot of willow clumps from the centre of the trail. I walked backwards indicating which clumps needed lifting, always in fear of tripping, being picked up in his bucket, and deposited in the windrow. I've been thinking a lot more about the arrangement for Sarah. I know it's important to have everything in place before she dies, if only to save the girls anxiety. Adam has been a great strength on the phone.

I've leaned heavily on my friends for help – something I'm not used to because I like to think I'm so strong and in control. But I'm not. I asked Eric Allen, a carpenter friend, to make a plain pinewood box with no frills or fancy work. He wept in gratitude at being asked. Philip Adams, an actor, is going to see to all the paperwork and stage-manage the farewell in Whitehorse before we take her to Atlin. I want it to be downstairs in the waxing room of the ski chalet where all the action is, not upstairs in the posh banqueting room – standing or sitting on the floor, no suits, no flowers. The quilt made for her by her quilting group will cover the table, and one of her quilts will drape the box.

It all sounds a bit cold and calculating, but it is a tremendous relief knowing that I've got friends looking after the details, and I need not be scurrying round at the last moment, and it'll make it easier for the kids to have everything taken care of. I tried talking to Sarah this morning, telling her she was going on a journey and for once I wouldn't be able to accompany her. She didn't rise to the cue. She still says she will get better and that this is just a temporary setback. Would that it were so. I don't feel the need to dispel the illusion and start talking to her about *death*. I feel sure she will do so, if and when she feels ready, and wants to. It's not for me to force the pace just so I can feel good about it, because that's what the books tell you to do. I believe she has her own agenda, and a solemn discussion about death is not on it at the moment. We hug a lot in bed at night, and I'm beside her all the time – precious moments.

I try to keep in the background in the day and disappear up to my ski trail in order to let the kids spend time with her. Yesterday she asked where I was, and Lucy said, "He's gone to build his ski trail." Sarah's reply – "Oh, he would, wouldn't he." I've had her to myself all that wonderful month in the UK. That was my farewell, and I do not need to hog her limited precious time now. I have eight hours of undisturbed hugging her during the night – so I'm very lucky.

31 Oct. '95

Sarah gets steadily more drowsy and confused. Her blood calcium is up, which may be making it worse. So one of the home nurses tried to put up a drip today to give Sarah a fancy new drug to lower her calcium, but her veins are so collapsed it wasn't possible to get a line in. Her doctor talked about putting an intravenous line in her neck, but I said No. I went out on my ski trail today and I thought, '…why should she have to go through any more medical interventions.' She went through chemo and radiation, she felt lousy and her hair fell out, and nothing made any difference. So why put her through one more thing 'that just might work'? No, we've got to let her go in her own way now and give her the freedom to die in peace.

She knows I'm here, I hug her and hold her hand all night long. I tell her I love her and she responds. We are ready for her to die; I think she's probably ready herself. As usual this is being run on her terms, and who am I to interfere? I've just rung Angus, wise Vancouver physician and dear friend, and he said I should let her go now. I can manage perfectly well myself. The girls are on hand, the two homecare nurses will come any time I need them. We are surrounded by friends, who smother us with love – and meals.

Adam is flying over on Thursday, and he will be a great support. I wish he didn't have to see his mum wasted, so he could keep the picture of her beauty at his wedding. Contrary to what I told him a week ago, I need him close by me. I'm all right most of the time; then I just cave in. I hate blubbering except with my close friends.

I think she knows she's started that special journey on which I cannot accompany her, as is my wont. I tried to talk to her about it two nights ago, but she didn't want to discuss it. We've been on so many journeys and adventures together it seems sad that I have to stand on the shore and wave good-bye to her on this one, with her knowing she's travelling off into The Unknown alone. We've been such balanced travelling companions. I do all the organizing and take decisions, but when the going gets tough it's she who comes to the fore with her eternal optimism that gets us through the most difficult circumstances.

Robert, I scribble whenever I get a moment. Please bear with me. I'm leaning on my friends unmercifully these days, and it's a wonderful relief to do so.

Letter #22

Whitehorse, 3 Nov. '95

My dear Robert,

Sarah is fading slowly, but there's an aura of peace over the house. Since our friends have taken over the nuts and bolts of the arrangements I have been much calmer. In fact, I haven't cried for a full 24 hours. The numbness has set in, as it has with every recurring crisis – a roller coaster we've ridden for the past 20 years, especially in the three since The Beast returned.

Sarah seems to be quite comfortable and in no pain. I've stopped giving her any medicine except Fentanyl patches. We can manage with the help of the two home care nurses, and there's absolutely no question of her going into hospital. Friends are being so supportive that all I have to do is ask, and the job gets taken over and looked after without another thought. She is so loved, asking seems to do friends a favour and allows them to do something concrete, rather than hanging around searching for platitudes to ease their own discomfort. Some cannot cope, their social skills not being up to it; others are solicitous in an unobtrusive way.

Sarah's special Atlin friend, Kathy, from Juneau, Alaska, is staying here, which spells me off for a few hours. I've got to get my strength up for the final lap. I keep going out to my ski trail every day, which gives me a couple of hours of utter peace in a place that has become like my own garden. Also it eases pressure on the house – a couple of people at a time around Sarah are ample. I've put a notice on the door asking visitors just to come in, give her a kiss, and then leave. She cannot converse, and trying bothers her. I hope the bluntness of my request doesn't offend, but this has to be done our way. This applies to all this business. It has to be done our way. I can't be thinking what is the 'correct' way of dealing with such a death. She's ours and we'll allow her all the dignity we can to die amid the peace and love of her own home surrounded by her family and friends.

Sarah is very weak, and helping her onto the commode has become a major performance now because she can barely stand. As I was lowering her onto the seat with my arms around her, the phone rang. "Fucking phone!" she said, clear as a bell, not having spoken anything coherent for a couple of days.

On Friday night I was awakened by Judith at 3 a.m. Some revellers returning from a party had noticed our garden fence on fire, and seeing the notice on our door, called Judith next door. I ran out in the -20C night in my dressing gown and slippers to find flames leaping 12 feet high from the fence around the compost. The woodpile against it was smouldering and about to ignite. How come? In the afternoon Idiot Me had emptied the woodstove ashes onto the snow-covered compost despite there was a perfectly good metal garbage can standing right beside it. When the wind got up in the night the fire took off. By mistake I heaved one log that cut the eyebrow of one of the revellers – on whom I had done a vasectomy a year ago. We dampened the flames a little with fire extinguishers until three fire engines appeared, lights flashing and sirens blaring. Bloody lucky because all of us might have been cremated if these houses weren't made of steel. Sarah must have really had premonitions as she lay in bed hearing all this palaver – like her favourite orgastic scene in *Like Water for Chocolate*.

4 Nov. '95

Sarah was awake in the night and vomited dry heaves. "Oh, I do wish I felt better," she said. That's the only complaint I've had out of her the whole of this trying time. What a woman! – as if I didn't know it before. I hugged her and told her I loved her for the umpteenth time. She looked me in the eye and said, in a weak voice, "I love you too." Those were the last words she spoke. But I have her in my arms in bed and can hug her and hold her hand and stroke her hair – what's left of it. I could never do that in hospital. She certainly won't go there so long as I'm around.

5 Nov. '95

I know she's dying. Perhaps she's across the divide already and all I am seeing is her stubborn physiology playing out its last macabre act. I wish she'd just let go because her laboured breathing is distressing for the children. I've seen this sort of thing before and am used to it, but they don't need to see their mother a shadow of her real self.

In the middle of the night her breathing is so shallow I'm sure she is gone. I decide, after long wrestling debate with myself, to give her all the morphine I have left in the ampoules in my black bag. When I've done it her breathing is not noticeably depressed, and this cruel charade is just the mechanics of her body from which her spirit has already soared.

8 a.m. I call the children over from next door to say their farewells. She's not giving up without a struggle. I just sit with her all day and hold her hand. As her breathing becomes more erratic I hold her chin up to keep her airway open and to stop the distressing croaking. At 3:07 p.m. she stops breathing.

I immediately phoned Gail, the home care nurse, although it's Sunday and she's off duty. "I need you," was all I could say; she was here in twenty minutes. We wrapped Sarah in one of her quilts and lay her under the beautiful one made by the ladies of her quilting group. The kids came in to kiss her. I thought they'd freak out seeing her dead; but they were marvellously composed, yet tearful. It was strangely peaceful to be in the house alone with her. But not alone, because Victor, our grandfatherly cat had sat on the bed with his head on her for the last three days, and lay on top of her all the time after she had died. I've always been a cynic about animals having 'feelings' – now no more. He knew something was up, and was a great support to us all.

On Monday morning the children, Alain and I went up Mount MacIntyre, the hill on the edge of the valley, to Father Mouchet's five-kilometre trail that we use for early season skiing. Six inches of fluffy new snow lay on the trees and bushes, and a bright, low sun cast eerie shadows. I've skied there many times but never under such beautiful conditions as that day. With the Yukon looking its proudest it was a perfect way for us to all be alone as a family, and to think and talk of Sarah.

It was a huge relief that I had leaned so heavily on my friends for help; Philip Adams arranged everything in Whitehorse and took care of the paperwork; Kate Fisher ditto in Atlin; Eric Allen, a carpenter/climber made a beautiful box out of plain pine wood he had salvaged from the town dump. Eva Howe and the girls decorated the ski waxing room with Sarah's quilts (she always did want a one-woman show). We laid her on the ski box covered with her ladies' quilt. I thought there would be a fair number of people but not the 100 who crammed in, those in front sitting on the floor. The kids and I greeted them as they arrived – I haven't had so many lovely hugs and kisses in one day in my life.

Father Jean Mouchet, who started the cross-country ski program in the Yukon, gave a very simple welcome in his heavily accented French voice. Audrey McLaughlin, Sarah's political boss, spoke briefly about 'friendship,' specially referring to Sarah. She gave some lovely tales about their holiday in Mexico where all the shopkeepers wept when she left because she had been such a good customer.

Adam read Shakespeare's Sonnet 33:

Full many a glorious morning have I seen
Flatter the mountain tops with sovereign eye,
Kissing with golden face the meadows green,
Gilding pale streams with heavenly alchemy;
Anon permit the basest clouds to ride
With ugly rack on his celestial face,
And from the forlorn world his visage hide,
Stealing unseen to west with this disgrace:
Even so my sun one early morn did shine
With all-triumphant splendour on my brow;
But, out, alack! he was but one hour mine,
The region cloud hath mask'd him from me now
Yet him for this my love no whit disdaineth;
Suns of the world may stain when heaven's sun staineth

Alain read his and Lucy's marriage vows in French. Judith and Lucy read from John Donne, as suggested by their Granny.

The dead and we are all under one roof... We think not a friend lost because she is gone into another land and into another world. No person is gone, for that heaven which God created and this world is all one world.

I then showed 80 slides of Sarah taken over the years, putting them through without any commentary, so they lasted about 15 minutes. The last two slides showed, first, Sarah looking at Cathedral Mountain, Atlin, from the prow of my sailboat; and finally her walking alone along a ridge in Scotland, aged 19 – off on another adventure, but alone this time.

Eric Allen, a Seventh Day Adventist, read the 121st Psalm.

I will lift up mine eyes unto the hills, from whence cometh my help.
My help cometh from the Lord, which made heaven and earth
He will not suffer thy foot to be moved;
he that keepeth thee will not slumber... nor sleep.
The Lord is thy keeper: ...thy shade upon thy right hand.
The sun shall not smite thee by day, nor the moon by night.
The Lord shall preserve thee from all evil: he shall preserve thy soul...
thy going out and thy coming in from this time forth, and even for evermore.

I read a Nepali love poem – *Eh Kanchha* – that Sarah and I used to sing with the coolies when we were in the Himalaya (the second verse is so bawdy it was unsuitable for such an occasion, though Sarah would have loved it):

Eh, Kanchha, malai sun ko tara kaslai deuna.
O Darling, please pluck a golden star for me

Tyo tara matrai hoina, sun pani kasai deula
Not only one golden star, I will pluck them all for you

Gai goru bandera, chittai betnu aunu
When you have tied up the cattle come quickly to meet me

Batoma rat par la, ujyalo me aunu.
On the way night will fall, so come quickly while it is still light.

Philip Adams read Gerard Manley Hopkins's *The Windhover*, my favourite poem.

I caught this morning morning's minion,
kingdom of daylight's dauphin, dapple-dawn-drawn Falcon,
in his riding of the rolling level underneath him steady air, and striding
High there, how he rung upon the rein of a wimpling wing
In his ecstasy! then off, off forth in swing,
As a skate's heel sweeps smooth on a bow-bend: the hurl and gliding
Rebuffed the big wind. My heart in hiding
Stirred for a bird, the achieve of, the mastery of the thing!

Brute beauty and valour and act, oh, air, pride, plume, here
Buckle! AND the fire that breaks from thee then, a billion
Times told lovelier, more dangerous, O my chevalier!

No wonder of it: sheer plod makes plough down sillion
Shine, and blue-bleak embers, ah my dear
Fall, gall themselves, and gash gold-vermilion.

Father Mouchet closed with a poem from the Wisdom of Solomon iii, I, (the last magical line about 'sparks among the stubble' being a bit reminiscent of the near conflagration two night previous).

But the souls of the righteous are in the hand of God,
and there shall no torment touch them.
In the sight of the unwise they seemed to die:
and their departure is taken for misery,
And their going from us to be utter destruction:
but they are in peace.
For though they be punished in the sight of men,
yet is their hope full of immortality.
And having been a little chastised, they shall be greatly rewarded:
for God proved them, and found them worthy for himself.
And in the time of their visitation they shall shine,
and run to and fro, like sparks among the stubble.

The whole farewell took about half an hour. Then Alain, Adam, Phil, and Eric carried Sarah out to our beat-up old Toyota, and we booted it for Atlin, five cars in convoy, in order to get there before sundown. It was a brilliant, crystal clear, sunny day with new snow on the mountains. We stopped for a brief picnic beside Little Atlin Lake because we were all famished.

We drove once round Atlin to reach the cabin for a biffy stop. Lori O'Neill had hung my flag at half mast. Then we headed out of town past the Old Pioneer Cemetery beside Peterson's Field airstrip, up to the new cemetery that lies on an esker overlooking Atlin, the lake, and all the big mountains beyond. It is a magical place. Forty or so people were waiting there for Sarah. She was carried in by Atlin friends, Herman Peterson, aged 81, among them. I would have asked Krist Johnsen (93) but I was afraid he might have dropped her.

Father Mouchet said a few brief prayers.

Kate Fisher read Shakespeare's Sonnet 116:

Let me not to the marriage of true minds
Admit impediments. Love is not love
Which alters when it alteration finds.
Or bends with the remover to remove:
O, no! it is an ever-fixed mark,
That looks on tempests, and is never shaken;
It is the star to every wandering bark,
Whose worth's unknown, although his height be taken.
Love's not Time's fool, though rosy lips and cheeks
Within his bending sickle's compass come;
Love alters not with his brief hours and weeks,
But bears it out even to the edge of doom.
If this be error, and upon me proved,
I never writ, nor no one ever loved.

Wayne Merry, a mountaineer, read "*I will lift up mine eyes unto the Hills*"; I read the Wisdom of Solomon poem that I learned as a boy when my parents died. The lake was steaming as it does before it freezes because of the cold water churning over and replacing the warmer upper water. The mountains looked quite ghostly in the fading light, with low shafts of the dying sun cutting across their base. New snow lay on every tree.

Alex McConnell had made a headboard from a stout piece of knotted pine with just 'Sarah Steele' carved on it. This farewell had so far seemed like a strange, disembodied dream, but was now for real and wrenched at us all drawing lots of tears. They lowered her into the cold ground ten feet deep and Father Mouchet said a final prayer. We each threw in some earth, and Ron Bowden did the rest.

We all adjourned to the Old Courthouse where Atlin friends had laid on a potluck tea. I showed the slides again, but in less sombre mood. Then Adam, Judith, Lucy, Alain, and I left for the cabin where friends had prepared supper for us. We all stayed down and watched *Like Water for Chocolate*, a welcome light relief. The moon was nearly full and unusually bright – Sarah's Moon, our friends called it. I slept in our bed in the porch where the window panes had frosty patterns on them. It felt very lonely. In its own special way it was a magical and fitting farewell to a very special lady.

So that's it, Robert, I hope I haven't bothered you with unwelcome detail, but I thought you would want to know because you'd have wanted to be there.

Letter #23

Atlin, 20 Nov. '95

My dear Robert,

Here I am in our Atlin cabin, sitting at the scrubbed fir table with the knobbly legs, surrounded by Sarah. Her vermilion appliqué of geese stands over the sideboard; behind me is a red, white, and blue *Flying Pinwheels* pattern quilt, one of the last she made; her miniature quilt of tiny squares is beside the door. I look through the living room to see, draped over a low easy chair, a blanket she crocheted, which grandson Tim likes to wrap himself in; an appliqué moose, my favourite of her handiwork and one of her earliest, is all puffed out with stuffing, sunrise beads in the left upper corner, a tree in the other, and at low-right under its bum a bunch of beads that represents a pile of moose turds.

She is everywhere – yet nowhere. Often in winter I have come down to Atlin for a night, just for a change of scene and for a little time on my own. Then I knew what to expect when I came home: "How's the road? Who did you see down there? Is there enough firewood? Did you remember to empty the kettle and remove the sink drain plug?" Now

I'll go home to an empty house (except for Victor cat, who will chide me for not taking him with me, as does Tim because they both love this place). It's two weeks exactly since Sarah died and the numbness is still there. I suppose it's some sort of physiological defense to protect me from going crazy with grief, and to save me the embarrassment of collapsing in a pool of tears every time anyone addresses me. I don't like the feeling of emptiness, as though my tear glands have dried up forever.

I came down alone yesterday afternoon. A few kilometres outside Atlin I ran into the forecast snowstorm. Darkness was falling fast so I turned left immediately on entering town and headed for the cemetery. I had to leave the car at the foot of the hill that climbs the esker because it was too slippery with new snow. So I walked up, big snowflakes catching on my eyelashes and dampening my hair. The mountains were hidden by the snowstorm. Light from the town shone orange below a layer of steam lying over Atlin Lake, which was churning as it does just before freeze-up.

Sarah's grave was covered by snow and the chunky pine headboard, with just her name carved on it, was crusted with hoar frost that I brushed away with my glove. I howled, as wolves do, a long plaintive cry in my aloneness. It was a relief to be so close to her, not because I could sense her lying in the cold ground in Eric's stout box ten feet below me: that was not her, just the vessel which carried her unquenchable spirit that was now soaring somewhere beyond those snowflakes and the mountains. Oh! How glad I am that we countermanded her will and buried her right here in what must be one of the most beautiful cemeteries in the world. The family has a place that will always be quiet, where we can visit at our leisure in total peace. What privilege and fortune!

People tend to turn to deep philosophy at times like this, trying to explain the unexplainable. Strangely, I haven't been bothered by the deeper meaning of it all – life after death, and all the stuff that religions make capital out of, and snare converts with. I do see her as being on a journey, heading off as we have so often done with only a vague idea of the destination (she usually with NO idea). Leaving the nuts and bolts to me, she would provide unfailing optimism to overcome. But this time she's alone.

I think there are some things in life – and especially in death – that we were never to understand. Were we meant to have all the answers this side of the grave? The religions would have us believe so and, if we believe hard enough in their own brand of dogma, all will be revealed. What bullshit! If God does exist – and I firmly believe s/he has a controlling hand in this massively incomprehensible universe we inhabit – why would s/he want her/his secrets out before the final climactic curtain call? A squib-like drama were it so. All I do know is that I can sense the very aliveness of Sarah – and the heavenly host, whoever they are.

This past two weeks there has been an amazing demonstration of love by the number of lives a very extra-ordinary person could touch. Of course, platitudes pour in at death, especially from people who feel they never paid enough attention during life. But there has been a huge outpouring of love for Sarah that has buoyed us all up: from her friends, naturally; from ex-booze and druggie clients; from pinko politicians, quilters, skiers, and just plain people off the street.

Some of the hardest calls have been trying to console inconsolables who have never learned to communicate feelings. They approach with long faces as I'm trying to cross the street, or worse we meet in the middle of traffic in a dash between lights – 'condolence in your grief,' 'sympathy at your loss,' 'so sad she has passed on' – all sorts of euphemisms that could be said wordlessly with a hug (perhaps not in the middle of the Main Street crossover). I don't want to sound churlish because everyone needs the chance to grieve a friend lost. I have tried my utmost to share the love around, but sometimes we have to laugh as she would have laughed.

The letters, however short, have been wonderful coming from all over the world, full of meaning with the occasional reminiscence that sheds yet another light on Sarah's character. Some cards have come off the 'sympathy' shelf at the local gift store, which must have been doing brisk business. The trouble is that in a small town like this there's only a small selection and we have many repeats of the few cards available. Pre-eminent are the heavily embossed white lilies (are they not an emblem of The Reaper?) that look vaguely obscene. The printed messages and poems that accompany the white lilies are grizzly, especially to a lover of words. I cut out the name and the message and put them in a basket in the hope that when I meet the person on the street I'll remember to thank them for their thoughtfulness. I guess it's the easiest way out for some people; it takes far longer to go downtown to the store and shell out a few bucks, when a couple of words on a sheet of writing paper would have meant as much, or more. I must stop being cynical and take them all for the tokens of affection they are. At least they have given us all a source of amusement besides one of gratitude for the very real show of love for Sarah.

The cabin is warm now that heat from the barrel furnace has seeped into the walls. I'm loath to leave and head back to Whitehorse on the snowy road, but I have lots to do there. I'm coming down to Victoria on 30 November to stay for ten days, as Sarah and I had originally intended. *Atlin's Gold* has arrived, sadly three days after Sarah died; but I did read it to her cover to cover during the past few months. Wow! What a stern and discerning critic she was. Caitlin Press has done a great job, and the cover is striking. I'll bring a copy when I come to visit you on Hornby, probably around 6 December. It is dedicated to Sarah and she would have been mighty proud of it – as am I after labouring over it for five years,

I went back up the hill to the cemetery this morning. Atlin Lake was steely blue, cloud hung over Atlin Mountain and Birch Mountain, and all the forests were clad in a new mantle of snow. What a beautiful place! But I have to go back to Whitehorse and face the empty house, which is perhaps the most difficult thing. When I walk in there will be no bed on the floor commanding the room. There will just be Sarah's photo with Jigme Taring's white *ashi kadar* scarf hung around it – a token of honour. What I miss most is doing things for her, impatient though I sometimes have been. She has looked after me for most of the past 34 years and allowed me to do many various and exciting things, whether together or apart. Being able to look after her for these months has been a privilege (if that's not too unctuous a word for it) and a joy to be able to return some small part of the care and love she has given so selflessly to all of us.

Letter #24

Whitehorse, 27 Nov. '95

My dear Robert,

Last weekend Lucy's husband, Alain, and I drove over to Haines, Alaska, to see the annual winter congregation of Bald Eagles. In full sunshine from Haines Junction we traversed the mountains and over the summit pass where the peaks stood out like Himalayan giants. Down on the Alaskan side heavy, wet snow weighed on the branches of the huge rainforest cedars and hemlock, quite different from the spindly pines and spruce on our side of the border. Gathered below Klukshu village in cottonwood trees that were rimed with hoar frost, eagles, perched in the bare branches, stood wrapped in black cloaks made by their wings. Salmon in the river writhed in their death throes after spawning, and an eagle would intermittently swoop down from a tree, haul the carcass out onto a sandbar, and peck it to pieces. The game warden reckoned there were 2,500 eagles that day, but the number can double in February.

We stayed the night in a motel and returned to the eagles before sunrise next day. When I got home I had the worst empty feeling of the past few weeks. I opened the front door and there was the couch where Sarah's bed had been with her photo pinned to the Afghan carpet on the wall above it. But she wasn't there to tell of our adventure, which I would normally have recounted in every detail. I knew the reality of her death would hit home soon, so I was expecting it. Oh! So empty, and me so empty of tears I could hardly cry for relief. I just sat and stared at her photo and felt immeasurably sad.

New snow fell while we were away, so I went up to ski the Sarah Steele Trail and took a cardboard sign I have made until the wood one is ready. I met Lucy up there after she had finished her training session, and we skied it together, twisty and interesting with a long rise through silver birch forest where the boughs were bent over with new snow. I had planned to take Sarah round the trail wrapped up on a sled behind a snow machine, like Zhivago's Lara.

I'm inundated by letters and cards; there's no way I'll be able to answer them all. I've sent my account of Sarah's farewell to several of our close friends, along with a photo, because they must feel cheated at not being there, and not having the chance to say good-bye. For us it's almost a feeling of relief that was helped by having such a wonderful farewell. I've never given much attention to the importance of rituals before, but now I see how crucial they are in coming to terms with grief.

It must be much more difficult when there's a sudden death with no time to prepare for it; when there's nobody to touch. I remember vividly, aged ten, my parents' deaths. My brother and I came home from school, and my father told us our mother had died. He'd already had her cremated and there was a bronze box on the lintel over the fireplace. As we knelt down I peeped through my fingers at the box and thought, 'Is that all that's left of my mother?' Then we buried her under a small tree at the bottom of the garden because, as a suicide, she couldn't go into a churchyard.

When my father killed himself six months later my brother and I weren't even invited to his funeral – presumably for fear of upsetting us. To this day I don't know what happened to him, or if there's a plaque on some cemetery wall somewhere to remember him by. I just recall our science master on a 'nature walk' telling the other boys that when someone committed suicide they were buried at a crossroads with a stake through their heart. No wonder my brother, who was just a teenager three years older then me, was fucked up by the experience. We were never able to talk about our parents together. It took so much longer to get over the whole traumatic episode than if we'd had a proper farewell.

VICTORIA, 9 DEC. '95

Sarah and I had planned to come down at this time anyway, mainly to take in Anton Kuerti's concert, to keep her appointment at the Cancer Hospital, and to visit friends. So I came anyway. Anton and I went for lunch and talked and talked. He told me he would dedicate, mentally, the slow movement of Beethoven's 2nd piano concerto to Sarah. What a fortuitous meeting in Atlin five years ago.

I then went across to Vancouver to do an interview with Vicki Gabereau about *Atlin's Gold.* Waiting in the CBC cafeteria felt a bit like before the viva of my final surgical fellowship. She was very professional and steered me through the half hour chat, which she played very straight and with genuine interest.

Then up Horseshoe Bay for the ferry to Nanaimo, and on to see you on Hornby. Another wonderful visit for which my deepest thanks. This time I was very conscious of the empty place at your table, and the absence of her laugh and argumentative chatter. Robert, I don't now how I'll make out over the coming year and more, but at the moment I feel fine – very sad of course – but fulfilled because we were able to give her such a send-off.

I'm convinced of the importance of a farewell – I use the word advisedly instead of funeral, which has such macabre overtones of men in dark suits, collapsible aluminium trolleys and plush-lined caskets with ornate handles. We made our farewell *our* way, and in that way (as you have so often told me) we let her go; nothing to hold her spirit back, but let it soar. William Blake wrote:

He who binds to himself a Joy
Doth the winged life destroy;
But he who kisses the Joy as it flies
Lives in Eternity's sunrise.

It seems to have taken the children in the same way, whereas I had thought they would freak right out. They've been magnificent – composed and stoic and very caring. We're all sad and tearful, but not paralysed. We talk and joke about Sarah a lot. The other interesting thing is that the room where she died, and the wax room at the ski chalet where we held the farewell, don't seem the slightest bit spooky as I thought they might.

So, dear friend, I must close this chapter now. It brings to an end this particular phase of our treasured correspondence that spans a year almost to the day. It has been such a help to write to you. I'll have to open a new chapter now and set off on my own road alone, as she has done, but it will be a very lonely road to follow. I'm going to miss her dreadfully. I'll end with the last paragraph of the piece I wrote about our journey round Patagonia together in which I am summarizing the things we'd take again when going off on our travels:

"What else have I forgotten? Oh, yes, it nearly slipped my mind while thinking of the minutiae of the journey. One travelling companion, forgiving when I am obstinate; cheerful when I am down; enthusiastic in sharing the joys and surprises a journey brings; tolerant when shown a dimly lit bedroom in a doss-house where the drains smell, sheets have not been changed for several passages, and cockroaches scuttle out of the shower; good-humoured when the train departure is delayed by half a day; optimistic when struck down by the runs; phlegmatic when robbed and it looks as if we're heading for the rocks."

Well, I have one such. To her, *mero jiban sati* – my lifelong friend – I owe all my thanks for another journey happily shared."

EPILOGUE

Robert Philips relaxing at home on Hornby Island

ABOUT THE AUTHOR

Retired doctor and mountaineer Peter Steele was born in England and lived in far-flung places such as Nepal, Bhutan, and Labrador before settling in Whitehorse, Yukon with his family in 1975.

Steele once ran the Grenfell flying doctor service in Labrador, travelling the coast by plane, dog team and boat. His first book, *Two and Two Halves to Bhutan*, tells the story of his young family's adventures in the Himalayas. He was Medical Officer to the ill-fated 1971 International Everest Expedition, an experience recorded in *Doctor on Everest*. He followed this with two books on medical care in the wilderness, and *Atlin's Gold*.

Eric Shipton: Everest and Beyond, a biography of the great British climber, won the Boardman Tasker prize for mountain literature. Steele's book, *The Man Who Mapped the Arctic: The Intrepid life of George Back, Franklin's Lieutenant*, won a Globe and Mail and Amazon.ca Book of the Year award.

His latest book, *And Far Away*, continues the memoir begun in *Over the Hills* and recounts his travel and mountaineering adventures.

Made in the USA
Columbia, SC
14 January 2018